Home Office

GW00541772

Prevention

Report of the
Advisory Council on
the Misuse of Drugs

London   Her Majesty's Stationery Office

Advisory Council on the Misuse of Drugs

Members

Dr P H Connell   Chairman

Dr T H Bewley
Mr J C Bloomfield OBE
Mr H E Carter
Mr D Cox
Miss P B Dempster
Miss A H Dixon
Professor R Duckworth
Professor J Griffith Edwards
Dr W W Fulton OBE
Mr A Gorst
Professor J D P Graham
Mrs A Jones
Dr D J King
Professor M H Lader
Dr G C Mathers
Professor W D Ollis
Mr G O'Connor
Mr M J Power
Mr B D K Price QPM
Mr S Ratcliffe
Miss G M Rickus CBE
Mr W E C Robins
Mrs R Runciman
Mrs M Sharpe MBE
Mr J A Smith
Mr G T Steele
Mr D Turner
Dr D Wild

Mr D J Hardwick   Secretary

Contents

i

Early Intervention

Education and Community Responses
  (a) Education of the community
  (b) Education of specific groups
  (c) Training of professionals

National Level
Co-ordination at an Intermediate Level
Co-ordination in Local Communities

Research on Supply
Research on Potential Demand
Research on Harm Reduction

List of Appendices

1 Introduction

Background

1.1 The Advisory Council was established by the Misuse of Drugs Act 1971. One of its responsibilities under the Act is to advise on measures to be taken for preventing drug misuse which is having or appears to the Council to be capable of having harmful effects sufficient to constitute a social problem. This report on the prevention of drug misuse has been prepared by a working group of the Council in accordance with that responsibility and has been endorsed by the full Council. The membership of the working group is set out in appendix A.

1.2 In the 1960s, misuse of drugs was largely confined to the London area. It has since spread gradually throughout the United Kingdom and must now be regarded as a national problem. Despite previous preventive effort, it is still on the increase, a trend which is reflected in most other European countries, and in many other parts of the world. In its report for 1982 (1), the International Narcotics Control Board noted that:

> "Despite the widespread awareness of the seriousness of the problems and the responses taken at the national and international levels, both regional and worldwide, the drug abuse situation continues to deteriorate in most parts of the world. The number of drug abusers is further increasing; abuse is spreading geographically; the number, variety and potency of drugs illicitly used are growing". (paragraph 7)

The Board also noted that "abuse of several drugs throughout Western Europe has markedly increased" (paragraph 95).

1.3 In the United Kingdom survey evidence to hand in the 1970s suggested that the total number of persons who had ever experimented with an illegal drug might amount to several millions; only a proportion of these go on to use drugs episodically or regularly, of whom some may subsequently develop problematic patterns of misuse (2).

---

(1) All references in this report are listed in appendix G.

1.4   A matter for particular concern is the increasing incidence of opiate drug misuse, as shown especially by the numbers of addicts notified to the Home Office and recorded in the Addicts Index. The most recent statistics show that in 1981 there was in increase of over 40 per cent, to 2,248, in the number of narcotic drug addicts notified for the first time to the Home Office, and that in 1982 there was a further increase of about 25 per cent to 2,793 (3). This compares with a figure of 800 for 1972. While these figures may have been affected to some extent by changes in the notification practices of doctors, data from other sources (eg. hospital emergency admissions, deaths) and non-medical evidence from the police, street agencies and others working with drugs misusers confirm a substantial and continuing increase in the number of individuals misusing drugs. Furthermore, the number of addicts notified to the Home Office represents only a proportion of the total population of drug misusers. Research commissioned by the Department of Health and Social Security suggests that the total number of opioid addicts in the United Kingdom may be at least five times the number notified.(4)

Scope of the Report

1.5   The increasing incidence of drug misuse casts doubt on the adequacy of existing preventive measures, making it more important than ever to examine their effectiveness and consider ways to improve them or develop better ones. There is , however, no simple solution. Ideally, we should be able to begin by identifying those measures which have been effective and those which have been less so. This is possible to a certain extent, and throughout the report we draw as much as possible on the available evidence. However, there is not always reliable evidence of the merits or shortcomings of any particular preventive measure and, even when there is, it may be dangerous to rely too heavily on such findings. For example, measures which have proved effective with one group in one part of the country may prove ineffective with an apparently similar group in another part of the country. The complex nature of drug misuse means that there are no simple solutions and that all initiatives should be cautiously undertaken, and monitored continuously as to their effectiveness.

1.6   For these reasons, this report seeks to identify the general principles upon which future prevention policy should be based, at both national and local level. At national level we have considered what specific measures, if any, should be employed. At local level we have been less specific and have sought to set out more general guidelines for the development of prevention programmes suited to the needs of particular localities. In drawing up our proposals we have taken note of recent reports on prevention of drug misuse prepared under the auspices of the United Nations and the Council of Europe (5 and 6).

1.7 Our concern has been to examine the theories which underlie the various approaches to the prevention of drug misuse, to describe the main options and identify those which we consider to be positively harmful, and then to make recommendations about the direction of future prevention policy. We have looked at the need to respond quickly to, or where practicable to anticipate, drug misuse by individuals, among particular groups or in specific localities. We have also considered the need to ensure the evaluation and monitoring of both existing and new approaches. It is important that responsibilities for the formulation, implementation and evaluation of prevention policy at national and local level should be clearly allocated and understood. We have therefore made proposals which build on the recommendations we have already made in our report "Treatment and Rehabilitation" (7) for a framework of services for those misusing drugs. Finally, we have examined the role of, and need for, research in relation to prevention policy and practice.

1.8 Our previous report on the prevention of drug misuse was specifically concerned with the needs of school children (ie those aged between 11 and 18) (8). In this report we broaden our interest and deliberately do not set out to confine ourselves to consideration of the needs of any particular group. Nevertheless, society is quite rightly concerned about the health and development of its young people and so their needs often feature prominently in many areas of social policy. Some measures to prevent drug misuse (eg statutory controls of supply) affect everyone in society, whereas others (eg education) may be more easily directed to specific accessible groups. Young people in their formative years are perceived as accessible by virtue of their attendance at schools, colleges, work experience and training programmes, and in social activities such as youth clubs etc. However, other social groups, to whom little attention has previously been directed, may be equally accessible and potentially more receptive. We have sought to identify such possible new approaches.

Readership

1.9 The problem of drug misuse and its prevention belongs to the community as a whole. As far as possible this report uses non-technical language in the hope that it will reach a wide readership and will stimulate informed public discussion and debate involving all those who are or may be concerned in the prevention of drug misuse. In particular, however, we would expect this report to attract the attention of members of voluntary and non-statutory agencies dealing with problems of drug misuse, and of local authority and health service administrators who would be concerned in the implementation of our recommendations.

Definitions of Prevention

1.10 Previous studies of the prevention of drug misuse have often adopted the following framework:-

a. primary prevention – the aim is to minimize the incidence of drug misuse;
b. secondary prevention – the aim is to reduce the present number of those dependent upon drugs;
c. tertiary prevention – the aim is to mitigate the effects of harmful drug use, usually through treatment, rehabilitation and social reintegration.

1.11 Although this framework has traditionally been applied to many medical and social problems, it did not appear to us sufficiently comprehensive for all elements of prevention policy, and we were therefore unhappy about adopting it as the basis for our consideration. In its place, we decided that we should concentrate on preventive measures which satisfied two basic criteria:-

a. reducing the risk of an individual engaging in drug misuse;
b. reducing the harm associated with drug misuse.

1.12 It is clear that not all preventive measures could be equally effective in terms of both criteria. For example, statutory controls aim to reduce the number of people who misuse drugs by making it more difficult to obtain them. These controls are an essential part of current prevention policy both in this country and internationally. However, the potential risk of such controls is that those who nevertheless misuse drugs may come to greater harm than would otherwise be the case. For example, illegal misuse of drugs in secret in order to avoid police attention or public disapproval may make it harder to obtain early assistance in the event of mishap. In this matter it is necessary to balance the interests of the majority who do not misuse drugs at all against those of the small minority who do. The general view, which we endorse, is that the preventive benefits of statutory control of supply outweigh the potential risk of increased harm to misusers.

1.13   As a necessary complement to control of supply a further important group of preventive measures aims at exerting direct influence on the level of demand for example by educational techniques. It is on the question of the objectives of drug education that the debate between reduction of levels of misuse or reduction of the levels of harm caused by misuse is most lively but we do not believe that a coherent prevention policy depends on all its measures being aimed solely at either reduction of misuse or reduction of harm caused by misuse.

1.14   Although preventive action by definition precedes what it is intended to avert, it is important to emphasize that the scope for prevention is not limited to the period before a particular drug misuse problem has arisen. Action taken to reduce the harm associated with drug misuse obviously has its effect in relation to those who are already misusing drugs, and may be taken both before and after they have begun to do so. There is also scope for intervention in the early stages of misuse, both to reduce harm and to prevent more serious problems from arising. There is some overlap here with the field of treatment and rehabilitation, but priority in the latter area is usually given to more developed and serious cases of misuse, and there is a danger that the scope for early intervention may be neglected. In chapter 4, therefore, we discuss briefly the requirements for action in this area.

Other Substances

1.15   Although tobacco, alcohol and solvents do not fall within the Council's remit, many of the measures examined in this report may also be of value in the prevention of the misuse of these substances and of other forms of harmful behaviour.

2   The Causes of Drug Misuse

2.1   The causes of drug misuse have been of continuing interest to policy makers and the professions concerned for most of this century, partly because of the expectations that, if a single cause or definable set of causes could be identified, then preventive efforts could focus upon reversing these causes and compensating for them.

2.2   There are many popular beliefs and myths about the causes of drug misuse. For example, it is widely believed that drug misuse involves young people only and is invariably associated with factors such as a personality defect, mental disturbance, ignorance of the damaging effects of drugs, broken family, bad company, lack of discipline or seduction by profession-al drug pushers. While there has been a considerable amount of research into why people misuse drugs, no single cause, or consistent pattern of multiple causes, has been identified. As Plant says (9): "There are so many types of drug user and so many types of drug that the profusion of different theories is hardly surprising." Plant also distinguishes, as we do, between factors influencing drug experimentation and those associated with persistent misuse.

Individual and Social Factors Influencing Demand

2.3   Among those who have studied drug misuse, there is widespread agreement that it is a complex social problem and not just a clinical or pharmacological one. In assessing all the evidence about causation, we have found it helpful to consider three approaches which can be applied to the study of social problems but are of particular interest in relation to drugs. They may be described as the public health, the psycho-social and the structural approach. Each of these approaches has made a contribution to the theory and practice of the prevention of drug misuse.

2.4   The *public health* approach focuses upon the interaction between drugs, individuals and the environment. Many drugs have a potential for misuse, at different times, by different people, for different reasons. No single psychological factor has been identified as the cause of drug misuse. A wide range of external "environmental" influences such as peer group, family, community, religion, sub-culture, may affect the drug/individual equation. To understand more thoroughly this complex form of social behaviour it is necessary to draw on social and developmental psychology as well as taking into account the effects of broader structural factors.

2.5 The *psycho-social* approach, which is most closely associated with post-war developments in health, social and moral education, emphasises the subjective meanings and rewards that individuals may find in their chosen drug experience and in participation in the "drug scene". Drawing upon the findings of developmental and small-group psychology, this approach emphasises the problems that individuals may experience when trying to satisfy the expectations of particular groups in society (eg family, peer group) or when adopting a new role (eg adulthood). This approach recognizes that the process of growing-up, both in terms of individual development and of having to assume an "adult" role, may increase the risk of drug misuse for young people. There are two main ways in which this may happen. In the first place, drug misuse may result from young people's awareness that they live in a society in which a variety of forms of recreational and medicinal drug use is accepted as "normal". In the second place, drug misuse may be a way of attempting to solve problems and of coping with the stresses and strains experienced in adapting to the complex demands of society.

2.6 Clearly an important unifying concept in this approach is that of "adaptation". The problems that individuals experience when trying to obtain a reasonable "fit" with their environment may stem from various aspects of growing up and at the succeeding stages of change: to adulthood, to middle and then to old age. Adjustments to changes in family relationships, to evolving personal and sexual identity, and later to loss and bereavement all present problems of adaptation, in response to which some people may seek the support they believe will come from taking drugs in an attempt to ease what they experience as unacceptable stress.

2.7 The *structural* approach attempts to understand the norms and patterns of behaviour developed by specific social groups as a response to their positions in the social and economic structure of society. Structural circumstances do not directly determine the probabilities of drugs misuse by particular individuals; rather they provide the context within which each social group develops its characteristic culture or subculture. Each subculture involves particular styles of involvement with legal and/or illegal drug use, which have to be understood if appropriate preventive measures are to be designed. A relatively recent body of social research addresses itself to this question (10), and some of its implications are being taken into account in cultural and community prevention strategies, and in health, social and life-skills education touching on drug misuse.

2.8 Membership of a particular social class, the opportunity or lack of opportunity for mobility between classes, wide differences in opportunity due to large regional variations in health and economic status, and many other "structural" factors, quite outside the control of the individual, are seen as major determinants of people's lives. The continuing inequality in our society places entire groups of the population at a grave disadvantage. To live in a deprived area, to be poor, to be a member of a minority group subject to discrimination, to struggle against the demoralising effects of long-term unemployment, all these situations are seen as a severe test of the ability to survive for long periods without chronic physical, psychological and social disability. Such forms of disadvantage are associated with various social and health problems, including perhaps those of drug misuse, though they may be only one group of precipitating factors, and there are, of course, many instances of drug misusers among all groups in society. It should also be noted that social and economic deprivation is likely to aggravate some of the deleterious effects of drug misuse.

The Supply of Drugs

2.9 So far this review of the various causes of drug misuse has been concerned with factors influencing demand. Although it is known that increased demand may stimulate increased supply, the reverse process may also be important and a readily available supply may create more demand. In one sense if there were no drugs, there could be no misuse. But since restrictions on supply normally have the effect of reducing rather than abolishing that supply, we have to consider the conquences of such reduction. In doing so, it is important to distinguish between the consequences of shortages of a drug upon levels of initial experimentation, and consequences for existing users (including heavy users).

2.10 Experience suggests that, when the numbers of existing users are low, as is the case with illegal drugs, an increase in the availability of drugs increases the opportunity for non-users to be offered a drug for the first time. Conversely, diminished supply may make existing users less generous in their offers to others when they have insufficient for themselves.

2.11   The mechanism by which non-users become experimenters is not very well understood, and may vary from one social group to another, depending upon the cultures and circumstances involved. But research (11) suggests that becoming an experimenter is an extended social process, involving first coming into contact with people who are using, then recognizing them as users, then being offered an opportunity to try a drug for the first time, then accepting one of these offers (not necessarily the first). These processes give rise to several groups – 'no contact', 'contact' (but no offer), 'offered' (people who have been offered a drug but not accepted it), and 'accepters' (experimenters).

2.12   The size of each of these groups varies a great deal from one area to another. One implication is that, just as it is misleading to put all users into one category (users may differ vastly in terms of frequency and level of use, drug used, circumstances, etc), so is it misleading to put all non-users into one category. The same research (11) showed that of all young people who were offered an illegal drug (mainly cannabis, stimulants and sedatives), on average about half accepted. This implies that in general levels of initial experimentation with drugs in relatively short supply are constrained by the level of that supply; but in the case of a substance which is already widely available, changes in availability will have little impact on the level of experimentation, since a marginal change in the rate at which established refusers of offers receive further offers is unlikely to disrupt their habit of refusal.

2.13   The consequences of changes in levels of supply for *established* users differ from those for experimenters. When supply is relatively easy (eg. alcohol), marginal changes in its availability (by an increase or decrease in the number of outlets or in prices) seem to produce corresponding changes in the total volume of heavy use in society (12). But when supply is 'tight', a slackening or further tightening of that supply may have more dramatic effects for established users: a slackening may lead some (at least) to increase their level of use quite considerably, whilst a tightening may lead to them 'switching' to a more freely available substance.

2.14   This phenomenon of switching may have severe consequences for health. When, for example, heroin supply falls users may swtich to other drugs which because of the form of the preparation or the degree of purity are more dangerous than heroin when injected. In the United States,

10

'Operation Intercept', a campaign to seal off the Mexican border and prevent marijuana entering the United States, is reported to have resulted in some marijuana users switching to a variety of more hazardous substances, and there was a wave of hospital admissions (13). In the United Kingdom there have been various campaigns at a local level to persuade shopkeepers not to display adhesives on their shelves, but there has been no detailed study of the extent to which this is likely to make sniffers switch to more hazardous products.

2.15   In general the effects of shortages of a particular drug are likely to depend on the availability of other substances, on the existence and attractiveness of alternatives to illicit drug misuse, which might or might not include medical treatment, and on various personal and cultural factors. Effects of tightening controls on the supply of drugs could include, as well as switching, adulteration of supply (leading to the additional health risks associated with use of impure drugs, and an increased possibility of accidental overdose when purer supplies are available), increasing prices (motivating more crime by addicts and increasing the rewards for pushers) and more full time involvement and effort on the part of addicts to secure supplies. Evidently, this is an area in which prevention policy must proceed with caution.

2.16   The likely effect of changes in the availability of drugs may be summarised in the following way:-

	Substance relatively freely available (eg. alcohol)	Substance in relatively short supply (eg. illegal drugs)
Effect of changed availability on initial experimentation	Slight	Considerable
Effect of changed availability on subsequent or heavier pattern of use	Moderate	Possibility of Switching

2.17   We believe that prevention policy must continue to include measures aimed at restricting the availability of drugs. It is mainly for this reason that statutory controls have been adopted in this country and many

11

other countries throughout the world. However, tighter controls in themselves are not the complete answer and it may also be necessary to examine more closely the ways in which the illicit drug market works and how it may be influenced. In this respect, it may be important to distinguish between the parts played by organised crime and by the activities of existing drug misusers. If, for example, existing misusers are primarily responsible for the spread of certain forms of drug misuse, the provision of adequate treatment facilities might reduce the number of such misusers and aid prevention by reducing the number available to recruit new misusers. In that context it is also appropriate to note that a key element in the so-called 'escalation' from initial misuse to long-term and potentially more dangerous forms of drug misuse is the individual's introduction to and association with a circle of existing drug misusers rather than the properties or effects of the drugs themselves (14).

2.18   A number of other questions might be asked. For example, why does the person who has drugs decide to give or sell these drugs to the newcomer? Is it more often a matter of giving or selling? Are there economic determinants related to the need to pay the rent or the desire to raise money to buy some more favoured drug, or is the drug deal much more based on the need for friendship and social cohesion? Does the market operate in a geographically haphazard fashion or is it prevalent in particular streets or areas? What effect does the condition of the national economy have on the size or activity of the illicit drug market (15)? We are not aware of any research findings which would have enabled us to answer these questions, and we believe that research in this area would be valuable.

Conclusion

2.19   There is widespread recognition that there is no single cause of drug misuse, nor can the influences discussed in this chapter be ranked according to their relative contribution to the total size and nature of the problem (16). We have not, therefore, based our recommendations on any single model of causation. The individual, social groups, structural determinants and the supply of drugs must all be taken into account when developing a comprehensive prevention policy. We recognize that we need to know much more about how these factors operate and how they may themselves be influenced (eg by education, the media, advertising, statutory controls, treatment etc).

12

3 Current Preventive Measures

3.1   In this chapter we seek to describe the range and nature of current preventive measures. It would clearly be impossible to identify and describe every single programme or specific project which directly or indirectly, deliberately or inadvertently, might have helped to prevent drug misuse. Our aim is therefore, to build up a general impression of what is at present being done to try to prevent drug misuse.

3.2   In chapter 2 we have shown that drug misuse is a complex social problem. No single cause or consistent pattern of multiple causes has been identified. Because there are many pathways leading towards drug misuse, some of which have not yet been identified or fully understood, there are a variety of potential preventive measures.

Broad Social and Economic Policy

3.3   We think it essential to recognize the relevance of policies which are directed towards the general wellbeing of society eg. measures for redistributing wealth, for varying the level of provision in areas such as health, education or housing, for reducing unemployment or for providing leisure facilities for the community at large. Such policies while not directly affecting the extent of drug misuse or determining measures for its prevention may nevertheless have some indirect effect, which may not necessarily be beneficial. It has long been recognized that social problems cannot be tackled in isolation because action taken on one problem could relieve or exacerbate another. It was for these reasons that the Central Policy Review Staff report published in 1975 (17) recommended better monitoring and co-ordination of social policy at all levels of government. Other reports (18) have recognized the links between social problems, and also the complex relationship between such problems and social or economic measures aimed at society in general.

3.4 However, it has not so far been possible to quantify the precise nature of these links or the multiple effects of any particular social or economic policy either in general terms or specifically in relation to the prevention of drug misuse. Nevertheless it is important to recognize that the effectiveness of the response to a particular social problem, such as drug misuse, is likely to be influenced by the responses to other social problems and by broad social and economic policies. Although these influences cannot be quantified the prevention of drug misuse must be seen as part of this much broader perspective.

The Availability of Drugs

3.5 The previous chapter identified the availability of drugs as one important influence upon both the levels and nature of drug misuse. For that reason, attempts have been made for many years to minimize this influence by the use of statutory controls.

3.6 By 1960, although there was little evidence of a serious national drug problem, there were various restrictions on the import, export, manufacture, sale, distribution, supply and possession of such drugs as opium, morphine, heroin, cocaine and cannabis. Possession of these drugs was restricted to people authorized by the Home Secretary and to patients to whom the drugs were supplied for the purposes of medical treatment. In 1961 an Interdepartmental Committee on Drug Addiction (the Brain Committee) (19) concluded that addiction to dangerous drugs was still very small and, consequently, that no new statutory controls were necessary. However, subsequent annual increases in the number of addicts to dangerous drugs, and changes in other factors such as the age distribution of addicts, resulted in the Brain Committee being reconvened in 1964. The Committee's second report, published in 1965 (20), concluded that trafficking in illicit supplies was negligible, and that the main source of supply to these new addicts had been overprescribing by a very small number of doctors. In response, the Committee recommended that the right to prescribe, supply and administer heroin and cocaine to addicts should be restricted. This recommendation was subsequently implemented.

3.7 The Misuse of Drugs Act 1971 consolidated the existing piecemeal legislation and established new and more extensive provisions for controlling certain drugs liable to misuse. This Act provides the framework of the present controls, of which the main elements are as follows:-

14

i. *Restriction of supply.* The general purpose of the controls is to confine the drugs to genuine medical use. The import, export production, supply and possession of controlled drugs are prohibited except for persons licensed by the Home Secretary and for those exempted by Regulation. Practitioners such as doctors, dentists, veterinary surgeons and pharmacists are permitted to prescribe, administer, manufacture, compound and supply most controlled drugs provided that certain record-keeping and safe custody requirements are observed. A special licence is required to produce, possess or supply those drugs, including cannabis and LSD, which have no established therapeutic use. In addition, doctors are required to have a special licence before they prescribe, administer or supply heroin or cocaine to addicts except for the purpose of treating organic disease or injury. Doctors are also required to notify the Chief Medical Officer of the Home Office of any patients considered to be addicted to certain controlled drugs.

ii. *Control of irresponsible prescribing of controlled drugs.* Since most controlled drugs can be supplied legally on prescription, it is essential that there should be some machinery to prevent these sources from being exploited. If a doctor or other practitioner has committed an offence under the Misuse of Drugs Act, or has been found by a tribunal to have been prescribing irresponsibly, the Home Secretary has power to direct withdrawal of authority to prescribe, administer, manufacture, compound or supply specified controlled drugs. The ultimate responsibility for the identification of cases of irresponsible prescribing and for taking appropriate action leading, if necessary, to tribunal proceedings, falls on the Home Office Inspectors. Although many of these cases arise as a result of their own enquiries, information is also received from the police, who have power to inspect the controlled drug registers maintained by pharmacists and so might discover evidence of irregular prescribing, and from other concerned organisations and individuals.

iii. *Enforcement.* Provisions designed to restrict the supply of controlled drugs would be rendered virtually ineffective if they were not adequately enforced. There are three main enforcement agencies. First, Inspectors from the Drugs Branch of the Home Office are responsible for ensuring that drugs are not diverted from legitimate sources (eg manufacturers, doctors,). Second, the police have responsibility for the investigation of the whole range of offences created by the Misuse of Drugs Act. Third, officers of the Board of Customs and Excise are responsible for the operation and enforcement of controls over the import and export of controlled drugs.

iv. *Penalties*. The extent to which the supply controls are observed depends, in addition to adequate enforcement, on the existence of suitable penalties for their infringement. Controlled drugs are therefore divided into three categories depending on an assessment of their potential harmfulness when misused. The maximum penalty for specific offences depends on the category to which the drug has been allocated. The highest maximum penalties in each category are for trafficking offences, the lowest for possession.

3.8 The extent to which the statutory controls act as an effective deterrent to drug misuse depends at least in part on the perceived chance of detection and conviction and on the scale of penalties which may be imposed. However these factors may operate in various ways and with different degrees of effectiveness on suppliers (at various levels), existing users (of various kinds), and potential new users. Their operation in relation to particular social groups may depend on broad cultural factors: for example the use of cannabis by some Rastafarians for religious purposes. A further question meriting investigation is the extent to which the criminal justice system may be used by drug users who have no other way to obtain treatment. Conversely, we have no doubt that the possibility, or fear, of criminal sanctions deters many drug users from seeking help from official agencies. However, as we have indicated above, (paragraph 1.12) we believe it is necessary to balance the interests of the majority against those of the small minority of drug users.

Educational Measures

3.9 In addition to trying to restrict the availability or supply of drugs, current prevention policy also includes educational measures which seek to discourage misuse. Such measures fall into three main categories, although there is, of course, considerable interaction between them:-

    a. education of the community;
    b. education of specific groups;
    c. training of professionals.

The following paragraphs attempt to provide a brief description of current practice in each of these areas.

(a) Education of the community

3.10 In this section of our report we are concerned with measures directed at geographically determined groups of people – at one extreme the entire population of the country, at the other the population of a single housing estate, neighbourhood or village. Such groups include people with a wide range of different and sometimes conflicting interests and views. Groups with common interests or views, whatever their geographical location are sometimes also called "communities"; these are considered in the section of this report on education for specific groups (paragraph 3.21).

3.11 The centrally-funded Health Education Council, which develops health education campaigns and initiatives within the broad framework of policies and priorities set by the Health Departments, has produced pamphlets on ways to help young people who take drugs and on the risks of careless use and storage of prescribed medicines, and an important element of its health education work in schools is the prevention of drug misuse. Nevertheless the individual forms of harmful behaviour to which the Council has given priority have been cigarette smoking and alcohol misuse either in isolation or as an element in its campaigns of broad health education designed to promote healthy styles of living (eg the "Look After Yourself" campaign, which focuses on diet, exercise, smoking and drinking). We understand that the Council feels that caution should be exercised in the use of widespread publicity on drug misuse, partly because of uncertainty over the size and nature of the problem in Britain, and partly because of the risk that ill-chosen educational methods attach disproportionate importance to drug misuse and arouse in some people an interest which they would not otherwise have felt. The Scottish Health Education Group has a broadly similar approach, and its activities to publicize its broad health education campaigns have included sponsorship of the Scottish Milk Race (for cyclists) and the Scottish Marathon.

3.12 Much of the in-service training of professional groups (paragraphs 3.37 – 3.49) provided by agencies such as the Health Education Council, the National Institute for Social Work and the Teacher's Advisory Council on Alcohol and Drug Education (TACADE) has a wider significance, since trainees are often influential in local communities. Also much of the supporting material and information provided by those bodies and others, in particular the Institute for the Study of Drug Dependence (ISDD), is intended for passing on either to specific groups, eg to school children, or to the community in general.

3.13 It is by no means certain that health education techniques used, for instance, in encouraging people to give up smoking or not to smoke in the first place, are applicable to the prevention of drug misuse. Health education is still an area of development and knowledge is only gradually increasing about how attitudes to social problems such as drug or alcohol misuse, and individual and social behaviour, may be influenced most effectively (see paragraphs 6.9 – 6.11).

17

3.14 In considering education of the community, it is necessary to consider also the role of the mass media. Although the mass media offer perhaps the quickest method of communicating with communities, whether nationally or locally, their use needs to be very carefully considered (21). So far they have not been widely used for official campaigns aimed at the prevention of drug misuse. Even if the mass media were used in this way, official messages would have to compete with independent contributions which have different, and sometimes conflicting objectives. For example, the media occasionally feature sensational and inaccurate reports about drug misuse. While the public generally may be knowledgeable about the subject, some irresponsible publicity may have adverse effects and even result in experimentation. In particular, sensational reports of the use of illicit drugs by well-known personalties may influence attitudes and behaviour especially of young people. The total output of the media neither can nor should ever be directly controlled and so the influence of such contributions must not be ignored.

3.15 However, the extent of the media's ability to formulate or change public attitudes is itself the subject of debate. Some experts in mass communication have moved away from a model of the media that emphasizes direct effects upon individuals, and towards the view that people *use* media, in selective ways, in ways that they find gratifying (22). The media's contribution may be to define issues for public debate ('setting the agenda') rather than to manipulate individual opinion (23). At the same time it seems likely that the media are capable of exercising a more direct persuasive influence on children than on adults.

3.16 The difficulties associated with using the mass media have, at least in part, led some to argue that direct appeals alone to individual members of the public through health education may not be appropriate as a means of curbing drug misuse. Efforts may also need to be focused on changing perceptions of misuse among influential sections of society, particularly doctors and the caring professions. An example of such an approach was the Campaign on the Use and Restriction of Barbiturates (CURB) mounted in the 1970s with the primary objective of reducing doctors' prescriptions of barbiturates. While it is hard to be sure of the extent to which the campaign contributed towards the continuing decline in the prescribing of barbiturates, it is even more difficult to assess whether, and if so to what extent, it changed the general prescribing practices of doctors or the expectations of the general public. However, we believe that there is now some evidence of public resistance to the use of drugs as the remedy for all illnesses or problems. Although this trend should not be

18

exaggerated, expert opinion in this country and abroad is tending to favour campaigns directed to changing the attitudes of caring professions, and thereby reinforcing the impetus for change in public opinion.

3.17 While it is important that drugs should not be seen as the solution to all illnesses or problems, it is equally important not to discourage the proper use of drugs. For example, the use, sometimes on a life-long basis, of anti-psychotic drugs and anti-depressive drugs, has revolutionized the management of schizophrenia, depressive illness and manic-depressive psychosis, often enabling people who would otherwise be in hospital to live and work in the community. Such patients have to be encouraged to continue to take their medicine regularly, perhaps for life; uninformed public attitudes and criticism which deters the proper use of such drugs or causes patients to refuse to continue with such treatments may cause a relapse, possibly with serious consequences such as suicide attempts.

3.18 It is important, therefore, not to condemn the use of all psycho-active drugs out of hand or to dismiss some people's reliance on them as pandering to weakness of character. Benzodiazepines are frequently prescribed for the treatment of anxiety on a short-term basis and used apparently without harmful effects sufficient to cause social problems of the severity of those arising from the misuse of, for example, heroin or alcohol. However, concern has been expressed both within the medical profession and by some women's organisations, among others, about the long-term prescribing of benzodiazepines, particularly to women. This, if prolonged, can lead to dependence and withdrawal symptoms. While on the one hand, the widespread prescribing of benzodiazepines may encourage the acceptance of drug taking as a normal way of life, thereby hindering the task of those who are trying to prevent drug misuse, on the other hand wholesale condemnation of all forms of drug use as a negative way of trying to cope with life's problems may discourage the appropriate use of drugs by those who have a genuine need for treatment.

3.19 The level and content of publicity about drugs within the community may also have some effect on the prevention of drug misuse. Such publicity is increasing, both in relation to preparations for the relief of headache, tension, and stress and in the promotion of new products. This may help to reinforce norms of drug use in our society which to some extent undermine the persuasiveness of health education.

3.20 Some argue that health education should promote positive and rewarding life styles rather than concentrate on ways of preventing or reducing risks to health. These approaches are not incompatible, and there are increasing attempts to link health education with recent positive trends in society, for example the growing interest in healthy diets and exercise.

(b) Education of specific groups

3.21 Educational measures in this category are those aimed at accessible groups or individuals considered to be either at most risk of misusing drugs or most receptive to educational techniques. Young people are generally considered to satisfy both criteria and so they have tended to become the focus of educational measures designed to prevent drug misuse.

3.22 It is for local education authorities, school governors and the schools themselves to decide whether, and if so how, to include drug education in their curricula. If they decide to do so, it is usually included as part of a broad programme of social education covering a number of issues such as exercise, diet, sex education, personal hygiene, alcohol and smoking. However, education aimed specifically at preventing drug misuse is not yet common because of the fear that it will promote experimentation.

3.23 Many primary and middle schools teach that pills and medicines should never be taken by children without their parents' knowledge and then only in the dose prescribed by the doctor. Much of this simple work is done in the context of science, home studies and healthy living linked with work on the human body and safety in the home. In relation to this and other work there is much evidence of situations being planned and used to encourage children to make informed choices about how, for example, their bodies interact with the environment and how choices open to them can affect their health.

3.24 The provision of health education in secondary schools is more complex. A growing proportion of schools teach health education through a composite course, for example, "Social Education" or "Citizenship", of which health education is an element. In some secondary schools these courses are provided for all pupils within years 3, 4 and 5, but they are sometimes also provided in years 1 and 2. These courses may extend and clarify the concept of the word 'drug' not forgetting the life-saving role of many, inform about the law relating to drugs and help in the understanding of the ways in which drugs affect the individual. In addition some courses attempt to help pupils to become more aware of and to cope with the pressure on individuals to experiment with alcohol, cigarettes and sometimes drugs. In many schools health education may also be part of traditional school subjects such as biology, home economics, religious education, physical education, English and social studies. In others, it is part of tutorial time.

3.25 A common teaching method is for the teacher to give an initial exposition, supported by a film or literature, followed by a question and answer session linked to written work often based on work-sheets. Other schools may show films and enlist outside speakers such as doctors or the police. Most lessons at present are directed towards increasing a pupil's knowledge and understanding of drugs and their effects on the body; some involve discussion methods to seek to establish decision-making skills and influence attitudes; recently a small number have begun to use situation simulation and role-play exercises to influence and reinforce decision making and attitudes. The potential value of small group discussion and simulation is widely recognized, but prior in-service training is essential even for those teachers who have the natural skills called for by these educational techniques. Moreover, the development of health education which includes these methods requires much planning and organisation. Vital elements in achieving this type of provision in schools are the leadership and support of the headteacher and detailed planning and organization by a senior member of staff.

3.26 Practical experience also indicates that it is important to employ a variety of teaching methods because individuals differ and the same message can affect each individual differently. For example, role play about how to refuse a drug or cigarette may help one individual, another may be helped by reflecting on what others say about drugs or smoking in discussion, another by a lesson on the effects of a drug or a cigarette on the body, another by advice or example by a respected person, another by personal experience of drug misuse or smoking-related illness in a family, another by the experience of success in some facet of his or her school life.

3.27 A few secondary schools embarking on social and political education are beginning to give consideration to the discussion of health issues over which there are strong differences of opinion and where questions of social and public policy arise. For example, should water authorities be required to regulate the fluoride content of public water supplies, and should there be more Government action to restrict the promotion of tobacco products or to reduce the consumption of alcohol?

3.28 A regard for health education in its widest sense may also be expressed through the whole school environment, the pattern of rela-tionships and routines established, and the self-esteem fostered among its

21

pupils. Common in schools, and important, though no one can measure their effect, are the right reassuring or explanatory words at a particular moment from a respected teacher to a pupil experiencing doubt or stress. In addition, health education is a much broader concept in schools than it was 15 or 20 years ago when it was associated more with hygiene, health risks and warnings. Breadth has been achieved slowly. Local education authority working parties on health education, curriculum projects and the initiative of schools themselves have all contributed. Now a growing number of schools, both primary and secondary, attempt to achieve a balance between aspects of physical health, hygiene and human growth and development, and the emotional and social aspects of life, and also to develop the skills and self-image which may lessen the temptation for pupils to seek confidence through drugs and alcohol.

3.29 Many secondary schools are well aware of the need to give consideration to education to equip young people to make the most of leisure time. The following extract from chapter 10 of the 1977 Department of Education and Science report, "Health Education in Schools" (24) is more pertinent than ever now with growing unemployment and the need to develop constructive leisure activities.

> "The indirect aspect of the teacher's work in the prevention of drug misuse – which he shares with parents and all others concerned for the welfare of growing boys and girls – is to create, so far as he is able, a climate which may at least make recourse to drugs less probable. It may be helpful, for example, in the school, as in the home, to give as much reassurance as possible in social situations. The belief of generations of teachers that they are right to encourage among their pupils constructive group activities which are not interfered with by adults may be reaffirmed".

3.30 A particular difficulty for schools carrying out educational programmes designed to promote healthy living and a sense of responsibility is the problem of children who are persistent non-attenders or who have had to be suspended because of bad behaviour. These children not only miss potentially beneficial influences and educational programmes but are also more likely to come into contact with and be influenced by those who misuse solvents. Persistent non-attendance is also a danger signal which may predict maladjustment in later life, possibly including drug misuse.

3.31 The youth service's preventive efforts are usually of a general nature although special efforts are made by individual clubs or projects in response to problems emerging in particular areas. The youth service makes two major contributions, especially in areas of high risk. First there are youth centres and clubs where drug misuse will not be tolerated and where there is active support and protection for those young people who do not wish to misuse drugs. Second the service provides agencies which seek to work with high risk groups and individuals by offering support and advice as well as social education and recreational programmes; but provision is very patchy. By providing both an alternative to drug misuse and support for those at risk the youth service provides valuable help for many young people.

3.32 Relatively few examples are documented of individual youth workers and units specializing in drug misuse, but there are workers (both "detached" and club based) mainly in inner city areas who work directly with those who misuse drugs. The youth service also occasionally supplies specialist workers at major events when drug misuse may occur (eg pop festivals). Most of the hundred or so youth counselling services also work with young drug misusers sometimes referring them to specialist agencies.

3.33 Most youth service agencies accept that their workers should acknowledge that the young people with whom they work might be misusing drugs and should be able to recognise such misuse when it occurs. Awareness of this kind usually requires training which, because of the large number of voluntary workers in addition to the much smaller number of professionals, frequently cannot be provided. The leader of an inner city youth club, although not condoning the use of cannabis, may be aware that some members regard it as culturally acceptable; but there are many clubs in which the problem either does not exist or, in the lack of appropriate training and experience, is not recognized.

3.34 Umbrella organisations like the National Youth Bureau, the National Association of Youth Clubs and National Intermediate Treatment Federation are able to provide workers with up to date information, publications and training courses as well as descriptions of current examples of work with young people at risk. Much of their work falls into the social education model which has a health education component, but more importantly they are in direct contact with face to face workers up and down the country, and although without specialist staff, they are in the best position to monitor new developments.

3.35 Although young people are clearly important, we are also concerned with other groups at risk of misusing drugs. In the 1960s and 1970s drug misuse amongst women was not considered an area of particular interest: a national survey conducted in the 1970s did not even differentiate between men and women (25). Researchers and policy makers have often assumed that hypotheses and policies drawn up in response to male drug misuse are equally applicable to women. The last five years have, however, seen increasing interest in women's use of legal (ie. prescribed) drugs (26). Also, the women's movement has drawn attention to the need to reconceptualize "social problems" (such as the drug problem) from the point of view of women's interests and position in society (27). It is estimated that literature on women and drugs now runs to about 200 published items (28). Much of this new literature has wide-ranging implications for prevention – as did nineteenth century women's temperance agitation.

3.36　We consider that this literature raises important issues not adequately dealt with in earlier, male-centred work. The potential contribution to drug prevention of women's consciousness-raising and self-help within the context of the women's movement, and the possibility that women's organizations may act as an alternative to problematic drug use, are areas deserving closer study.

(c) Training of professionals

3.37　In chapter 8 of our report "Treatment and Rehabilitation" (7) we noted that there was a shortage of suitable training for the wide range of professionals involved with the treatment and rehabilitation of problem drug takers. There is an even greater shortage of training to equip appropriate professionals to prevent drug misuse, since what training is currently provided is related mainly to the treatment and rehabilitation of those already misusing drugs.

3.38　So far as health care professionals are concerned, their training at student, postgraduate or in-service level includes little or no material on either the prevention of drug misuse or the means of dealing with drug misusers in a way which will minimize harm, other than the immediate physical ill-effects, to the drug misuser, to his or her immediate family and friends and to society. Furthermore the health care professions, because they often have ready access to drugs, are at particular risk of themselves becoming misusers. So far as we area aware, they receive little or no education aimed specifically at helping them to recognize and avoid this risk.

3.39　Police officers receive instruction about drugs during their probationary period (first two years) at both District and Force training schools. At District level the curriculum is recommended by the Home Office and is mainly concerned with the law relating to the misuse of drugs. At Force level they receive further instruction on the law and time is allowed for them to discuss with drug squad officers the practical problems of dealing with drug misusers. In the course of their careers, all officers are likely to receive further education about drugs. In England and Wales, senior ranks attend various courses at the Police College, Bramshill and similar regional establishments, whilst junior ranks attend various courses at their Force training schools. In Scotland, most forces provide training in drug abuse, and courses on the subject are given to detective officers attending the Scottish Police College. Some of these courses will have time devoted to an examination of the law dealing with drug misuse and there will be discussion on the practical problems of dealing with drug misusers. These discussions are most likely to involve drug squad officers who have, over the years, acquired a large reservoir of knowledge from their experiences of dealing with drug misusers. In general, however, most police officers in the United Kingdom receive little or no training that might foster an increased awareness of the complex causes of drug misuse and the various ways in which they might contribute to preventive efforts in the communities they serve.

3.40 The greater part of police work connected with the misuse of drugs is handled by drug squad officers. Officers selected for these squads receive their training at selected police training schools. The courses provide instruction on both the practical and theoretical aspects of drug investigation, and include lectures on drugs legislation and operational matters such as surveillance techniques, practical search procedures, the use of information and many other subjects which are of importance to officers working in this particular area. The intention of the courses is that each student will have gained sufficient knowledge of the drugs legislation and practical expertise to enable him to deal efficiently and effectively with all types of drug related investigations. The detailed content of these courses can vary from one training school to another. However, we understand that some courses include material on the medical and social aspects of drug misuse, although again it is not clear that this will necessarily cover the prevention of drug misuse.

3.41 Teachers are trained either by means of a one year postgraduate certificate of education course following a normal degree course or by means of a 3 or 4 year BEd degree which combines a degree course and practical teaching experience. Each training institution, in association with its validating body, has considerable autonomy in deciding the form of the course which it provides and information is not available centrally about the precise detail of the content of every component or every course. The general impression is that, with very few exceptions, the training institutions have until very recently provided little in the way of education for drug prevention. This is not perhaps altogether surprising. Both kinds of training have a great deal of ground to cover and are constrained – especially in the case of the post-graduate certificate of education – by the time available: and many teachers will never be required to deal with drug prevention. For both these reasons there may be the view in the training institutions that drug prevention is a matter which might be better left to in-service training.

3.42   Courses of in-service training for teachers are provided by universities, polytechnics and colleges and by HM Inspectorate in nationally published programmes and, more locally, as a result of Department of Education and Science regional courses. Although detailed information on the subject matter of the courses is not available centrally, the prevention of drug misuse is likely to occur as a topic in courses where counselling, guidance, pastoral care or health education is a main subject. In addition, local courses, seminars or meetings may be arranged specifically on drug misuse prevention. One of the foremost voluntary organisations in this field, TACADE, estimates that in the UK between 2,000 and 3,000 teachers a year may be involved in in-service training in education for drug prevention.

3.43   The initial training courses for youth workers are of 2 years duration with up to 50% of the time devoted to supervised field work. Course content varies and is often student-directed to a considerable extent. Work on drug misuse may arise through students' experiences during field work, because an individual student selects the subject for an essay or special study or because a student group elects to study the matter. Although there is no reliable information about the frequency and quality of such activities it is a reasonable assumption that the matter is not wholly neglected in initial training because it is recognized that many youth workers will have to deal with some form of drug misuse at some stage in their working lives.

3.44   There is no formal requirement or nationwide scheme of in-service training for youth workers. However, youth service journals carry articles on drug misuse, advertise short courses and provide details, sometimes summaries, of the relevant literature. Individual youth services conduct their own in-service courses, particularly when some manifestation of drug misuse is a matter of local concern. Again, it is not possible to quantify such activities because they do not occur on a regular basis.

3.45 Social workers (including probation officers) receive minimal information and training about drug problems on their professional qualifying courses, although some students will acquire valuable experience and training when on student placements in specialist drug agencies such as clinics or rehabilitation projects. Most training on drug problems for social workers in the United Kingdom is provided on an ad hoc basis as part of in-service training, dependent on the initiative of training officers, employers or other staff identifying a need for more knowledge about drug problems. This tends to be given more attention by the probation service in England and Wales because of statutory duties concerning probation orders for drug offenders. Until recently social service departments had limited contact with drug problems and were therefore less likely to identify training needs. However, the continuing pressure on social services to provide a service for the younger solvent sniffers has led to a greater awareness of the wider problems related to drug misuse experienced by some clients and requests for more in-depth training about both drugs and solvent problems.

3.46 To date it is extremely difficult for training officers to obtain expert advice and help in setting up short courses, while few are willing or able to teach the subject themselves because of lack of experience of the client group. The majority tend to rely on the more conventional but increasingly out-of-date course model of inviting medical and social work 'experts' from the drug field to contribute to a one or two day event. Unless the speakers are familiar with the problems of the course members and are able to provide material that assists staff to plan their work more effectively, this approach may reinforce assumptions that drug misusers can only be dealt with by specialists. A programme composed mainly of formal lectures rarely allows time for experimental learning or enables trainees to explore their anxieties and diffficulties about working with drug problems. Some authorities have resolved the problem of providing in-service training by employing an experienced trainer, with specialist experience in the drug field, to act as course tutor. They have then been able to design a course that provides basic information about drug problems and examines methods of working that have relevance to local problems and resources. This seems to lead to a more integrated course programme and allows for greater flexibility in teaching methods.

3.47 From time to time specialist drug agencies such as drug clinics or non-statutory organisations such as Lifeline in Manchester may assist in providing short in-service training courses for local social work staff, but these generally only occur in areas where there are staff suitably trained and specifically employed to develop training.

3.48 Since 1979 the National Institute for Social Work has provided three to four day residential and non-residential multidisciplinary courses (generally 1 to 3 per year according to demand for places) attracting a high application rate from probation officers and field and residential social workers. These are run by specialist staff employed on a freelance basis, while the courses are administered by the Institute. These courses aim to provide a broad orientation in the theory and practice of work with drug and solvent problems. There is a strong emphasis on encouraging trainees to feel more confident in adapting their generic casework and counselling skills to work with this client group, and on the demystification of preconceived ideas and fears about drug misusers. While there was some difficulty in recruitment for residential courses at times of cutbacks in local authority training budgets during 1980, this does not appear to have been a significant problem in recent years as most courses have been oversub-scribed (each course takes 30 people). Applicants come from all over the United Kingdom indicating a severe lack of local in-service training provision. Many are expected to assume a specialist resource role on returning to their employing authorities and to assist in planning in-service training for colleagues.

3.49 Apart from the training provided specifically for members of individual professions, there is some multidisciplinary training, primarily in-service courses. However most of these courses are organized on an ad hoc basis, and the number of places available is far too small to meet existing demands.

4 Future Prevention Policy

4.1   In the previous chapter, we have given an indication of the nature and extent of the measures currently employed to prevent drug misuse in the United Kingdom. In this chapter, we seek to identify some general principles upon which future prevention policy, both at national and local level, might be based. Before doing so, however, we think it essential to highlight some of the problems of taking action to prevent drug misuse. These factors must be kept firmly in view when considering the recommendations contained in the remainder of the report.

4.2   Although our review of causation in chapter 2 was necessarily brief, there can be do doubt that the factors and influences leading to drug misuse are complex and to some extent unknown. This has two important consequences for prevention. First, it is exceedingly unlikely that there is some unique preventive measure which, once discovered, could prevent all drug misuse. It is far more likely that, as at present, a number of different measures will have to be used in an effort to tackle what are considered to be the various causes of the problem. Second, since the causes of drug misuse are not fully known, there is always likely to be scope for improving the effectiveness of existing preventive measures, in the light of advances in the understanding of causation. However drug misuse involves decisions and choices by individuals, and it is unlikely that any set of external factors, other than complete suspension of supply, would in itself be sufficient to ensure its total prevention.

4.3   For these reasons, and in the current state of knowledge, any proposals for future preventive measures need to be advanced with a certain degree of tentativeness. On the other hand it would be irresponsible to do nothing until we were satisfied that the problem was fully understood. That happy position may never be attained. What can and should be done is to learn from experience and to proceed with caution. This is the philosophy which has guided us in framing our recommendations.

4.4   An additional problem is the inherent difficulty of assessing the effectiveness of a particular measure, or combination of measures, designed to prevent something happening. There is no means of being certain what would have happened if no preventive measures had been taken or if some other approach had been adopted. On the other hand, if there is a change in the level or nature of drug misuse it may be very difficult to attribute it to any particular measure.

4.5   In these circumstances it would be wrong to conclude that all prevention has so far been ineffective even though, as we noted in paragraph 1.2, the incidence of drug misuse is still increasing. However, there is a great deal more which can be done, despite all the difficulties, to evaluate the effectiveness of preventive measures. The real problem in the past has been that evaluation has rarely been considered, let alone actually attempted. This is an important matter to which we refer in chapter 6, where we discuss the type of evaluation which might be attempted.

4.6   Whilst keeping these general considerations in mind, we now turn to consider the main elements of future prevention policy.

Future Social and Economic Policy

4.7   The first element is the contribution made by broad social or economic policies. We identified and briefly discussed the influence of these policies in paragraphs 3.3 and 3.4. It is not possible to predict every consequence of any particular social or economic policy. Even if it were, it would probably still be necessary to choose between conflicting objectives and consequences. Nevertheless, although the precise mechanisms are not properly understood, there is a relationship between the prevention of drug misuse and the effects of broad social and economic policies. In some cases that relationship may work in favour of the prevention of drug misuse. At other times, it may make the task of prevention even more difficult.

4.8   While we accept that it may often be impossible for the formulation of broad social or economic policy to take account of all the potential consequences, if known, for the prevention of drug misuse we nevertheless fully support previous reports which have recommended improved co-ordination of social and economic policy formulation. In paragraph 2.8 we considered some of the structural factors which influence patterns of involvement with drug use in individual social groups and sub-cultures.

Economic management, tax and benefits structures, and policies on health, social services, education and the "family" all have an obvious bearing on the formation of these structural factors. They are also seen as having direct effects on individuals who for example become unemployed as a result of economic recession, or do not have access to adequate leisure amenities, education opportunities or social services because of the restrictions on public spending. Although direct causal relationships cannot often be established, we believe it is essential that the effects of broad social and economic policy on the structural context of drug misuse and on individual attitudes are recognized. The implications of this should, we believe, be taken into account in the allocation of resources at national level both to specific prevention activities and to related areas such as health education.

4.9   We also believe that measures aimed specifically at the prevention of drug misuse need to take account of and, as far as possible, anticipate the effects of the main social or economic policies. In some cases it might be appropriate to seek to re-inforce a particular policy, whilst in others it might be necessary to try to mitigate those effects considered particularly harmful to the prevention of drug misuse. In general, the success or failure of preventive measures needs to be assessed against this much broader perspective.

The Availability of Drugs

(a) Statutory controls on supply and possession

4.10   In the previous chapter we noted that statutory controls were the main method at present used in attempting to restrict the availability of drugs. We consider that these controls, particularly over illicit importation and supply, will continue to make an important contribution to the prevention of drug misuse. We regard the effectiveness of the police and HM Customs in this area as essential to our prevention strategy.

4.11   We have previously examined several aspects of the statutory controls and we regularly review the need for controls on individual substances. For example, we have previously recommended that certain barbiturates should be controlled. All the evidence which has since accrued has supported the case for this recommendation and we hope that it will soon be implemented. We also undertook a full review of the classification of drugs and of penalties under the Act which was published in 1979 (29).

4.12 In our report "Treatment and Rehabilitation" (7) we considered how the prescribing of controlled drugs could be improved and included proposals for amending the statutory controls (chapter 7 and recommendations 24–25 – see appendix E). While those proposals were aimed primarily at ensuring that those already misusing drugs received appropriate treatment, they are equally relevant when considering the prevention of misuse, since it is clear that in some instances drugs prescribed to addicts are finding their way on to the black market. Another recent report has examined all aspects of the security of controlled drugs, including the need for new or amended statutory controls (30).

4.13 The statutory controls mentioned above are aimed at those drugs considered to have the greatest potential for misuse. However, we consider that it is necessary to take a somewhat broader view and to consider the availability of drugs in general. There are other drugs which, although not subject to the special controls mentioned above, still have some potential for misuse. Furthermore, we consider that the general use and availability of medicines in society may have some influence on drug misuse. It is at present difficult to substantiate that the level of drug misuse is directly linked to the quantity of medicines consumed by society as a whole. On the other hand, we believe that the prevention of drug misuse can be made more difficult if the widespread use of medicines for therapeutic reasons, in many instances for relatively minor illnesses or disorders, is generally accepted in our society. For these reasons, we consider that statutory controls over the availability of drugs need to be reinforced by other means which we discuss in the following paragraphs.

(b) Influencing public attitudes towards medicines

4.14 A prime responsibility for combating undue reliance on medicines rests with health professionals, particularly doctors. Many patients feel that they have not received proper treatment unless medicines have been prescribed, even for minor illnesses. Health professionals can therefore play an important role in educating the general public on the proper use of medicines, both by restricting supply to cases where there is a clear need and by ensuring that their patients understand the reasons for this. Attention might be given to this in training, a topic which we discuss further below.

4.15 A related issue is the advertising of medicines. There has been little research on the relationship between drug misusers and advertising to the public of "self prescription" medicines. One piece of research suggests that TV advertising has no measurable effect (31). We are however in no doubt that advertising can help to promote the view that all health problems can be cured by the use of the right medicine. In the climate of opinion thus created, the task of dissuading those who might be inclined to experiment with drug misuse is made more difficult. We note that advertising to the public of medicines available over the counter is opposed by the Pharmaceutical Society of Great Britain because it undermines the professional advice available to the public from pharmacists when purchasing medicines. We therefore welcome the strict controls that exist over the advertising to the public of medicinal products.

4.16 As far as medicinal products available only on prescription are concerned those which are most promoted by way of advertisement or otherwise tend, as is to be expected, to be those newly brought on to the market. Under the provisions of the Medicines Act 1983, any new medicine has to satisfy strict criteria on quality, safety and efficacy before it can be put on sale. In our view there is at present a proper emphasis on safety, but this may lead doctors when presented with a new drug to suspend their own clinical judgement as to what is the most effective treatment in any given case. It has been claimed that the system does not prevent the introduction of new drugs with little or no therapeutic advantage over existing drugs, or even those of less efficacy and safety than existing products (32). In Norway the drug licensing authority has to be satisfied that there is some medicinal or economic justification for marketing a new drug (33). We think there is a case for further strengthening of the licensing provisions along these lines.

(c) The role of treatment

4.17 In the course of our review, we also considered the potential role of treatment as a means of restricting the availability of drugs. We have already noted that initial drug misuse is usually the result of an offer from an existing misuser (see paragraph 2.11). Although a number of other influences are clearly involved it is reasonable to suppose that the number of existing drug misusers could have some effect upon the rate at which new misusers are recruited. Successful treatment of existing drug misusers, resulting in a reduction of their numbers, might therefore in turn reduce the rate of recruitment of new misusers. This relationship does not appear to have been researched, but we believe it is likely to exist and is probably important. Our previous report (7) noted that existing treatment facilities were inadequate and made a number of recommendations which we hope will effect an improvement. We consider the full implementation of those recommendations to be urgently necessary not only in the interests of existing misusers, but as a means of preventing the recruitment of new misusers.

4.18 The methods of treatment of drug misusers also affect the availability of drugs. There is evidence of some spill-over of drugs prescribed for addicts. If, for example, an addict has methadone prescribed for him by a doctor treating him, he may choose to supply some or all of it to others. This can be a lucrative practice. We reaffirm the recommendations in our report on Treatment and Rehabilitation (7) that guidelines on good treatment practice should be drawn up, that there should be an early extension of the regulations which restrict the right to supply or administer certain drugs to addicts (other than for the treatment of organic disease or injury) so as to include all opioids, and that greater use should be made of the tribunal machinery established under the Misuse of Drugs Act to deal with irresponsible prescribing (chapter 7 and recommendations 23–26 – see appendix E). As a result of these recommendations a medical working group has been set up by DHSS to consider both the preparation of guidelines and the extension of licensing restrictions, and we understand also that a number of doctors have been subject to tribunal proceedings for irresponsible prescribing. We welcome these developments.

Early Intervention

4.19 In paragraph 1.14 we mentioned the importance of action taken in the early stages of drug misuse problems. There are two main aspects of early intervention. The first involves early intervention in individual cases in an attempt to reduce the harm caused by existing misuse and to prevent further misuse. Intervention of this kind largely depends upon all professionals being properly trained to recognize drug misuse at an early stage and respond appropriately. Our recommendations in paragraphs 4.46–4.51 below on the training of professionals are therefore also relevant to the development of effective early intervention. In this context, we reiterate the view expressed in our previous report (7) that treatment facilities should adopt a multi-disciplinary and flexible approach, taking full account of the range of services available from both statutory and non-statutory bodies (chapter 6).

4.20 The second, but closely related, aspect of early intervention is the need for local communities to be able to react quickly to, or if possible anticipate, local drug problems. This depends not only on professionals being well trained, but also on the existence of a permanent framework for co-ordinating local services, professionals and non-statutory agencies in conjunction with local community associations and bodies such as parent/teacher associations, and sharing resources of information and experience. This should provide the basis for effective monitoring of local drug problems and for mounting integrated and well-informed responses.

4.21   We discuss in the next chapter the practical details of such a permanent framework. However, to be effective, it will be necessary to establish an improved database at both local and national level as recommended in paragraphs 6.19 to 6.21 of our previous report (7), with increased use of small local studies to establish local needs.

Education and Community Responses

4.22   In chapter 3 we noted that there were three main categories at whom education might be aimed: the community, specific groups and professionals. Before considering future policy for each of these categories, it may be helpful to draw a distinction between the different educational approaches most commonly used separately or in combination when teaching about many health and social topics, including drugs.

4.23   When applied specifically to drug misuse, these approaches may be summarized in the following way:-
– emphasis on the drugs which are misused and on their effects
– emphasis on the individuals who misuse drugs
– emphasis on the situations in which decisions to misuse drugs are made
– emphasis on the cultural use of drugs.

4.24   None of these approaches can be used in every situation, nor should any of them be discarded. The question of which approach, or combination of approaches, should be used in a particular situation will have to be determined by those responsible for providing the education, in the light of a careful assessment of their particular needs and objectives. The formulation and implementation of effective and co-ordinated prevention policies also raises organizational questions which we consider in more detail in chapter 5.

4.25   In deciding which approach or combination of approaches is most suitable for specific situations, the following points might be borne in mind. Whilst we accept the need, in appropriate circumstances, for education to include factual information about drugs and their effects, we are concerned about measures which deliberately present information in a way which is intended simply to shock or to scare. We believe that educational programmes based on such measures on their own are likely to be ineffective or, at worst, positively harmful; there may, however, be scope for the use of such measures, where appropriate, in individual counselling.

4.26 Furthermore, we do not accept that educational programmes based only on the provision of accurate factual information about drugs and their potential dangers are sufficient to prevent drug misuse. It is now generally accepted that knowledge of itself does not usually change attitudes, far less alter behaviour (34). It is important, therefore, that information should be used carefully in conjunction with other educational approaches. For example, our examination of the causes of drug misuse (chapter 2) suggested that social and cultural factors were of considerable importance. It appears, however, that drug education in the past has failed to recognize the importance of these factors, or has underestimated them. As the causes of initial or occasional drug misuse come to be better understood and the responsibility for future prevention policy more clearly defined (see chapter 5), we expect that drug education will increasingly adopt techniques which focus on social and cultural factors. In chapter 6 we consider the need for evaluation of the effectiveness of health education programmes.

(a) Education of the community

4.27 Bearing in mind our definition of community (paragraph 3.10), education might be tackled at a number of different levels (eg national, regional, district, local etc). However, we do not consider that education of the community should aim specifically at reducing the incidence of drug misuse. As we have already noted (paragraph 3.13), there is still much to learn about how attitudes and, more importantly, actual behaviour can be influenced most effectively. Evidence is now accumulating on the effectiveness of anti-smoking campaigns but it is by no means certain that such techniques are appropriate to the prevention of drug misuse where there is a much greater risk of stimulating interest where none previously existed.

4.28 For these reasons, we consider that broad health education campaigns are probably the best method of seeking to prevent drug misuse amongst communities at whatever level. As a general rule, we consider that as the size of the target community increases so a broader educational approach will need to be adopted. We have identified three main levels at which education of the community might be attempted – national, district and local.

4.29 *Education of the community at national level.* For the reasons outlined above, we support the use of broad health education campaigns. The precise nature of such campaigns raises questions about health education in general which are largely outside the scope of this report. Nevertheless, we consider that campaigns which promote the safe and appropriate use of medicines may help to prevent many forms of drug misuse. We also favour the use of projects which seek to encourage healthy life-styles by means of active public participation eg sporting events.

4.30 Although we do not favour national drug education campaigns, we would like to see more basic drug education material produced centrally. It is clearly important not to stifle local initiative, but without a certain amount of accurate source material there is a danger that local education programmes will not be soundly based. There are already a number of national bodies which produce a wide range of factual and educational material. For ease of reference, these bodies are listed in appendix B. We suggest that these sources are used when local drug education projects are being considered or whenever reliable information about drugs is required.

4.31 In paragraph 3.14, we discussed the media's influence on drug misuse. Although their precise effect is unclear, we are in no doubt that informed and balanced reporting can assist in the prevention of drug misuse. Equally, we are in no doubt that sensational or inaccurate coverage can hinder effective prevention. For that reason we have given some thought to ways in which the media can be helped and encouraged to achieve and maintain a more constructive approach. This is clearly a very sensitive matter for there can be no question of seeking to interfere directly in the issues which the media choose to report or, in the final analysis, the way in which items are reported.

4.32 However, an important factor in achieving good quality coverage of drug issues is to ensure that the media have access to a wide range of independent, authoritative information and expert opinion on drug matters. So far as information is concerned, we hope that the media will make full use of the sources identified in appendix B. As regards expert opinion, there are several national organizations which, if asked to do so, could suggest independent, authoritative expert contributors for articles or programmes about drugs. Some of these bodies are listed in appendix C which we hope the media will also use when expert advice or contributions on drugs matters are required.

4.33 *Education of the community at district level.* A number of important administrative responsibilities relevant to prevention are located at levels intermediate between the national and local community levels; in particular, it is at this level that resources are allocated by the various statutory agencies. District health authorities and local authorities responsible for personal social services and education should therefore assess the needs of their areas. In the light of that assessment they should review the availability of resources, both statutory and non-statutory, and ensure as far as they are able that suitable prevention programmes are developed, either general programmes aimed at healthy living, or more specific programmes tailored to the current pattern of drug misuse in their areas.

4.34 In chapter 5 we make specific proposals for the effective co-ordination of this work, and the involvement in planning of the relevant agencies. We would hope however that at the same time close informal links at working level between the agencies will be strengthened, not least to ensure a proper balance between education aimed at the community and education aimed at specific groups within the community. In a few areas initiatives promoting such multidisciplined co-operation have developed. We welcome these, but recommend that they should be extended to include the public to a greater degree in planning of services and the care of misusers. Through the experience of such partnerships a concern to prevent will develop, and should be supported by resources and health education skills when the area is ready for it.

4.35 Local radio and television also have a significant part to play in educating the community in regions or conurbations. For example, social action broadcasting, which has been developed recently with considerable success in many parts of the country, offers a means of focusing public attention on social problems and promoting various forms of community involvement (35).

4.36 *Education of the community at local level.* Here is the possibility of the greatest impact, and prevention of drug misuse should be part of a wider objective of achieving a healthier community. Such topics as drinking, smoking, exercise, diet, drugs are all concerned with individual and cultural ways of life. The recent Council of Europe report on prevention supports the view that changes in life styles locally follow from the real involvement of the total local community (36).

4.37 An emphasis on local participation and partnership is embodied in some recent thinking about the planning of the personal social services and the role of the "voluntary" sector; the following trends are particularly relevant, and offer scope for improved prevention.

(a) The "patch" system of social services aiming to engage local inhabitants in providing support (37).

(b) The Barclay Report "Social Workers – their Role and Tasks" (38) recommends the creation of community social work which has the dual responsibility for counselling individuals and families with problems and undertaking social care planning to mobilise local resources of "people and pounds". The latter involves developing prevention by creating community networks to improve life by friendship and concern to all living in any given neighbourhood.

(c) The informal sector of care includes relatives who frequently undertake massive and continuous support to the disabled and handicapped – emotionally and physically. Much greater efforts are required to contact and support the relatives of drug misusers.

(d) Self help groups – a more literate, healthy, and mature society now expects to be included in discussion and decisions affecting their lives. There is much lip-service paid to consultation but less real partnership from the initial planning stage of any service or capital development; but whenever a lead is given, substantial numbers of any community respond. In the absence of such professional initiatives many groups of ordinary people have formed support services for children, the handicapped and the elderly. Groups of this type, catering for drug dependants or their relatives, have been set up in a number of communities, eg Tranx, Narcotics Anonymous and Drugline. The social services departments should in future plan jointly with such community groups to provide a caring fabric in each neighbourhood.

4.38 We would have liked to have been able to give examples of local experience in trying to respond, successfully or unsuccessfully, to the problems of drug or solvent misuse. A few initiatives have been brought to our attention, but as far as we are aware no comprehensive up-to-date survey of local experience in this field exists. We recommend that such a survey should be compiled.

(b) Education of specific groups

4.39 There are a number of specific groups for whom it might be considered particularly desirable to provide health education which includes the prevention of drug misuse as one of its objectives. Although the precise content of such education may vary from one group to another, we consider that there are certain general principles applicable to all groups.

4.40   We believe that the aims of education are twofold: (a) to reduce the recruitment of individuals into patterns of drug involvement that involve illegality and (b) to reduce the proportion of those taking drugs (legal or illegal) who suffer medical or social harm. We believe that these aims are compatible but recognize that, in practice, particular educators and programmes will focus primarily on one or the other. The importance of keeping both in view is that any evaluation of education (whether involving judgement or research) should address itself to both aspects. It would not be a positive outcome of education for example, if a small reduction in drug use was achieved at the expense of a significant increase in medical or social harm amongst those remaining users.

4.41   Drug education as such should be de-emphasized as a separate topic area, whether in school curricula, other institutions or the mass media (national or local press). Whenever possible, education about drugs should be integrated into broader frameworks of health and social education.

4.42   Decisions about which specific groups should receive particular attention must be made locally. However, we recommend that young people should not be regarded as the only target group. There are many other groups for whom action to prevent drug misuse might be considered eg professional and management trainees, middle-aged women, the unemployed, pregnant women, the old-aged.

4.43   In establishing educational responses it is important to recognize the needs and receptivity of differing groups. Some, eg women in antenatal care and school children, though generally low risk groups, may be easily accessible and potentially more receptive to general health education. Others, including older adolescents, at higher risk to substance misuse, may more readily be approached through programmes within youth training or work experience schemes.

4.44   The education of adults could proceed through existing frameworks related to health and safety at work, or be integrated with existing alcohol education programmes. These have been set up in many areas, with the support of the trade unions and management. Many primary health care teams have established preventive education groups, often allied to screening procedures, or directed to specific patient groups. This approach, encouraging patient participation, could reach a wider population. Such groups, eg specifically aimed at young mothers or the elderly, could play an important preventive role, both by alleviating the stress and loneliness they may experience, and also as a forum to discuss appropriate drug use.

40

4.45   Programmes directed to specific groups can only be effective if they are supported by community consensus. By utilizing existing frameworks a wider population can be involved. Linkage of programmes, addressed to differing groups, eg school children and their parents, requires careful planning and cooperation between agencies, to provide consistency and reinforcement of the approach.

(c) Training of professionals

4.46   Our review in chapter 3 of the training currently provided to equip professionals to prevent drug misuse suggests that the present coverage is patchy and, in some respects, quite inadequate, although we welcome the contribution made to the in-service training of certain professional groups by non-statutory agencies such as TACADE and the resources for multidisciplinary training produced by ISDD. While this is only one training need amongst many we nevertheless believe that it should now be given higher priority in view of the recent escalation in problems of drug misuse.

4.47   Such training should have two main objectives. The first would be to teach appropriate professionals how to educate specific groups of the kind identified above, so that they will develop appropriate attitudes and will be properly trained in the necessary techniques. Second, those same professionals, and others whose work may bring them into contact with drug misusers, need to be trained to respond to drug misuse in a way which will minimize harm to the drug misusers, to his or her immediate family and friends and to society. Teachers, youth workers, police officers, doctors, nurses, social workers and probation officers are examples of the types of professionals who should receive education about drug misuse for both of these reasons. At the introductory stage such training might well be interdisciplinary, but it seems likely that the potential for involvement of different disciplines would need to be followed up in separate sessions.

4.48   Our proposals here should be read in conjunction with those in chapter 8 of our previous report (7) for the training of professionals who work with, or may in the future encounter, drug misusers (see appendix E, recommendations 27–37). The implementation of those proposals should in itself provide a sound basis for training the professionals concerned in preventive skills. Accurate factual knowledge about drugs and drug misuse, for example, is essential not only in relation to the treatment of drug dependence but also to facilitate early intervention in individual problems of drug misuse and reducing the harm associated with drug misuse. However, training in preventive skills obviously involves certain

41

important additional elements, and although the need for involvement of a wide range of professional groups applies to treatment and rehabilitation as well as to prevention, in the case of prevention the emphasis lies on different disciplines. Some professionals, such as health education officers, whose involvement in treatment and rehabilitation is relatively minimal, play a leading role in prevention. A further difference lies in the degree to which training in prevention can, or should, be focussed specifically on drug misuse. Many of our recommendations would not be consistent with a training approach which dealt with drug misuse in isolation from all other health and social problems.

4.49   We have not attempted to determine in detail the contents required for a programme of training in preventive skills, partly because these would obviously need to vary for different professional groups, and also because in view of the uncertainty about what is effective in preventing drug misuse, there is considerable room for experiment in the field of training. However, it is essential to draw on existing experience, knowledge and skills, and to enable professionals to learn from these, using participative as well as didactic methods. We suggest that the following are among the elements which might be included:-

(a)   teaching methods for decision making, self-monitoring and inter-personal skills, and ways of raising self-esteem, pastoral care skills and requirements for onward referral, identifying and managing drug problems;

(b)   consideration of theories and explanations of drug misuse, public and professional attitudes to drugs and drug misusers, attitudes towards other statutory and non-statutory agencies, and ways of working in co-operation;

(c)   information about current trends in drug misuse, the effects of drug misuse and about drug misusers.

4.50   Obviously the selection and balance of these elements in any training programme should take account of the differing needs of the various professional groups: for example, primary school teachers should normally require only a basic minimum of training, but at the secondary and tertiary levels much more thorough training is appropriate especially for teachers who adopt a specialized role in preventing drug misuse. For most health professionals it seems appropriate for training in prevention to be weighted towards early intervention and reducing the harm associated with misuse, rather than primary prevention.

4.51 We recommend that all bodies responsible for the initial training of teachers, youth workers, police officers, doctors and other health professionals, social workers, probation officers, health education officers and any other relevant groups should consider the case for providing basic programmes of training in preventive skills, tailored to the needs of each professional group. However, we do not intend that such training should take the place of in-service training, often of a multi-disciplinary nature, which is currently provided. Continuous in-service training has been made more important by the everchanging pattern of drug misuse, though lessons previously learned are still of value provided the professionals concerned can be trained to apply the basic understanding to the new situation. We therefore welcome moves to provide back-up materials to those who may be in a position to influence or have a responsibility for in-service training courses and we recommend that the appropriate authorities should support such courses by releasing practitioners to attend them.

5 Responsibility for Prevention

5.1 In earlier chapters we have drawn attention to the increase in drug misuse, described existing preventive measures and made a number of recommendations as to ways in which some of these can be developed. Local and individual initiatives have brought about significant improvements in the past and will continue to do so. However we doubt whether sufficient impetus can be given to new initiatives without a greater degree of co-ordination than exists at present. In this chapter therefore we consider how responsibility for determining and implementing prevention policy both at the national and at the regional or district levels should be allocated. By "prevention policy" we mean a consistent framework of principles or guidelines within which a range of measures of prevention should be devised.

5.2 We have said that drug misuse is a complex human problem and that neither its causes nor its remedies are likely to be straightforward. It follows, in our view, that no attempt should be made to restrict responsibility for prevention or regard it as a particular form of specialism. The comparatively widespread availability of harmful drugs and the difficulty of predicting or accounting for the incidence of misuse make it a matter of concern to society as a whole. As we have indicated in the two foregoing chapters, there is a wide range of different existing or possible preventive measures which may contribute towards the prevention of drug misuse. The parties who are or might be involved in implementing such measures include parents, education and training agencies, health education agencies, social workers and probation officers, youth workers and youth organizations, law enforcement agencies, the health care professions, employers and trade unions, the pharmaceutical industry, the media, and Government. Moreover not all the activities which can contribute to prevention of drug misuse need be aimed specifically at this problem. We therefore consider that, while there is a clear need for some preventive measures to be co-ordinated, it would be unduly narrow to conceive of any single agency being given full responsibility for all measures of prevention, either nationally or locally, or to regard the major responsibility for prevention as being either a national or a local one.

5.3 We nevertheless consider that it would be desirable for certain aspects of prevention policy, primarily in the fields of education, training and community responses, to be more actively sponsored and co-ordinated than at present, and that this responsibility should be specifically allocated at the national level and at a more local level. Equally there is a need for co-ordination and for an improved flow of information between these levels. Policy trends must be communicated outwards from the centre; but if policy is to have a firm factual base, there must be a flow of information towards the centre on patterns of drug misuse and on trends in practice and the development of responses to drug misuse. One of the difficulties we have faced in our study has been to establish with any degree of certainty the extent to which local communities are responding to the problem of drug misuse and the measures they are adopting (see paragraph 4.38). While any attempt to co-ordinate prevention policy must take account of existing resources of experience available in voluntary and statutory agencies concerned with the provision of education and social services, it is vital that new insights and initiatives should be developed in response to problems of drug misuse.

National Level

5.4 As a relatively recent DHSS discussion document recognizes "there is an important Government role in creating the conditions and climate of opinion which make local effort effective, or in some cases possible" (39). In the field of prevention of drug misuse we believe it is for the Government to determine an overall framework of policy within which other bodies at both national and local level can make an effective contribution. Other bodies can contribute to these tasks but prevention must on occasions be a political issue and therefore one on which ultimately the government of the day must take decisions. In addition, there are a number of specific ways in which the Government is able to assist prevention. These include:-

(a) stimulating initial and in-service training;
(b) promoting the production of suitable educational materials for primary prevention;
(c) promoting the availability of information on national and local aspects of drug misuse;

(d) fostering an integrated and effective research response ensuring that such studies are successfully addressed to policy considerations and brought to the attention of those working in the field;

(e) monitoring changes in drug misuse prevention measures.

5.5 At present, although the Home Secretary has a certain overall responsibility throughout the United Kingdom on general matters relating to drug misuse, no single Government Minister has a specific co-ordinating responsibility in relation to its prevention. Instead responsibility is effectively split between the Departments concerned with the different aspects of prevention. The Home Secretary is responsible in England and Wales (and in some respects, Scotland) for the scope, effectiveness and enforcement of the statutory controls in the Misuse of Drugs Act. In England, education is the responsibility of the Secretary of State for Education and Science, and health and personal social services the responsibility of the Secretary of State for Social Services; in Scotland and Wales the respective Secretaries of State have responsibility for these matters, and in Northern Ireland they are the responsibility of the Department of Health and Social Services, Northern Ireland, and the Department of Education, Northern Ireland, which are also at present subject to the control of the Secretary of State for Northern Ireland. When jointly considering prevention and health these last four mentioned Secretaries of State and their Ministers concerned are collectively termed the "UK health Ministers". Several other Ministries have responsibilities which may be relevant to prevention, for example schemes providing opportunities for employment or voluntary work beneficial to the community, such as the Community Programme and the Voluntary Projects Programme, which are administered by the Manpower Services Commission on behalf of the Secretary of State for Employment, or the Urban Programme for which the Secretary of State for the Environment is responsible.

5.6 Thus in any part of the United Kingdom a number of different Secretaries of State have responsibilities in respect of drug misuse prevention. We recognize that this is unavoidable; indeed in many respects it is entirely appropriate since it would be unrealistic to attempt to divorce responsibility for prevention measures undertaken by a particular sector, say education, from ministerial responsibility for that sector. However it reinforces the necessity for effective co-ordinating machinery. In order therefore that the various elements of prevention may be co-ordinated within a consistent policy framework, we recommend that one government minister should assume specific responsibility for the co-ordination of prevention policy at national level.

5.7 A number of considerations point towards choosing the Home Secretary for this task. In addition to having a general co-ordinating role, the Home Office is responsible for the only substantive legislation relating specifically to the misuse of drugs (the Misuse of Drugs Act 1971), and, in particular, has the specific function of overseeing the control of the supply of drugs which we take as the basis of preventive measures. On the other hand, the Home Office lacks established day-to-day relationships with those working in the fields of education, health and social services, and these activities, at national level, are the responsibility of a number of other government departments. Nevertheless we believe that it would be more appropriate for the Home Office to assume the lead responsibility for co-ordination at national level in relation to prevention of drug misuse than for any of those other Departments, which have more specific roles in relation to their own aspects of prevention.

5.8 We recommend therefore that the leading role in respect of prevention policy should be assumed by the Home Secretary. His general role in relation to drug misuse should in future embrace a specific responsibility for the co-ordination of prevention policy as distinct from its implementation, which will inevitably remain the responsibility of many Government Departments and other agencies. In the exercise of this responsibility he should maintain close liaison with the other Departments which we have mentioned.

5.9 We consider also that there is a need for a suitable forum to enable national organizations concerned with the prevention of drug misuse to come together to exchange views and experience. While the Advisory Council might be able to bring such bodies together on an ad hoc basis it would not be appropriate for it to do so on a regular basis. We therefore recommend that the Home Office, in the co-ordinating role which we have recommended in the preceding paragraphs, should examine ways in which such a forum might be established.

Co-ordination at an Intermediate Level

5.10 While it is possible to devise at national level an overall framework of prevention policy, this is unlikely to be effective in the absence of a more localized structure for the development of prevention practice and the co-ordination of relevant services. This structure needs to be capable of a flexible response to local variations in conditions, and of doing justice to local experience and initiatives and to the work of voluntary and non-statutory organizations who are responsible for much current preventive activity. The structure also needs to be capable of taking account of existing responsibilities, in health and local authorities, for health education, general education and personal social services, and of effective communication and liaison with these bodies. It should, therefore, be based at a level intermediate between central government and the local community*.

5.11 The general functions of the structure we propose can be summarized as follows:-

(a) drawing together all strands of existing prevention practice, promoting liaison between the various statutory agencies and between them and the voluntary sector;
(b) identifying the problems in relation to drug misuse;
(c) suggesting preventive measures and encouraging their promotion and the provision of the necessary resources by the relevant authorities and agencies.

5.12 In particular the following specific tasks among others should be attempted:-

(a) encouraging and co-ordinating education of local communities in general and of specific groups, and promoting liaison between local authorities and health authorities in the field of health education;
(b) encouraging and facilitating the training of relevant professionals;
(c) developing and supporting facilities for advice, counselling and early intervention at local level to tackle drug related problems;
(d) influencing general social policies at local level in order to take account of drug misuse.

5.13 Many different disciplines and agencies will need to be involved, some statutory and some voluntary, in this work of co-ordination. In our report "Treatment and Rehabilitation" (7) we concluded that the health service region had a major role to play in the provision of services relevant to treatment and rehabilitation. However, in relation to prevention we do not see the need for a co-ordinating body at regional level; the primary need is for co-ordination at a more local level at which local authorities, district health authorities and voluntary agencies can liaise effectively together*. This should not preclude the possibility that regional personnel,

---

* A minority of the working group which prepared this report and of the Council do not agree with some of the conclusions expressed in this section. Their views are set out in appendix D.

including members of the regional drug problem team, as recommended in paragraph 6.7 of our previous report, might assist more localized prevention activities from time to time. Good liaison will also be necessary with the authorities responsible for funding education, social services and health services at the appropriate level.

5.14   Again in our report "Treatment and Rehabilitation" (7) we considered the need for co-ordination in areas smaller than regions, and concluded that there was a need for local drug advisory committees which could bring together the various interests. Because we considered it essential that a specific individual should be given responsibility for initiating action to establish such a committee, and because the district was a suitable local unit, we recommended in paragraph 6.11 of that report that the district medical officer should be given this task.

5.15   We note that in some parts of the country co-ordinating committees of this nature were established some years ago, sometimes on the initiative of the health authority or the police service, sometimes as sub-committees of the joint consultative committees set up with the encouragement of the DHSS to promote liaison between local authorities, health authorities and local voluntary organisations; some of these committees are already active in considering and co-ordinating prevention activities.

5.16   We have considered whether these existing and proposed committees might provide a suitable basis for area co-ordination of prevention. However, since our proposals for drug advisory committees were formulated with treatment and rehabilitation in mind, the lead responsibility and membership are concerned with the delivery of services. Membership of a co-ordinating body for prevention, on the other hand, should reflect a broader range of interests, laying greater weight on the concern and responsibility of ordinary citizens, teachers, youth and community workers, and others. It will not always be appropriate for health authorities to take the lead: this depends on local circumstances and needs. We are also conscious of the fact that our proposals in our earlier report are still the subject of consultation with various statutory and voluntary agencies and interested organizations. There appear to be three possibilities, therefore:-

1) to reformulate the aims, responsibilities and membership of the proposed drug advisory committees;
2) to establish separate co-ordinating machinery for prevention;
3) to consider at a future date proposals for co-ordination of prevention in the context of whatever structure may be adopted as a result of our earlier proposals for drug advisory committees.

5.17 Co-ordination of prevention by committees established under the auspices of the district health authority might have a number of implications:-

a) there could be a tendency towards undue emphasis on psychiatric and drug treatment specialist perspectives on prevention – which might prove unacceptable to many prevention and education workers;
b) local authorities which have responsibilities for education and personal social services usually cover a larger geographical area than district health authorities; both responsibilities are of vital importance in developing prevention strategies;
c) the development of strategies for the prevention of drug misuse could be divorced from general trends in health and social education in schools, further education institutions and the community;
d) local authorities tend to have closer relationships with local communities, and with local voluntary bodies, and activities of voluntary and community organizations and associations thereof do not necessarily correspond with health authorities boundaries.

On the other hand:-

e) a separate co-ordinating committee for prevention activity might lead to wasteful duplication of effort: the need for knowledge of local drug trends and resources would be common to both;
f) prevention activities would be considered against the general background of drug misuse in the district, and could be effectively co-ordinated with other services for drug misusers;
g) there is no other existing co-ordinating committee to which responsibility could be given; the setting up of another ad hoc body could be time consuming and expensive.

5.18 On balance we have concluded that there should be one committee only at this level; and that the proposals in our earlier report (7) for the setting up of drug advisory committees form a basis on which to develop this new, more broadly based dual-purpose advisory and co-ordinating committee with an extended function in the field of prevention[*]. Paragraph 6.14 of that report reads as follows:-

"As to the membership of district drug advisory committees, those who form the regional drug problem team and, if one exists, the district drug problem team (paragraph 6.15) will have an important part to play, together with representatives of statutory and non-statutory agencies providing services for problem drug takers. In addition the following, or their nominees, may have a useful contribution to make either on a regular or occasional basis:

Health Service: District Medical Officer
General practitioner nominated by the Local Medical Committee
Pharmacist nominated by the local Pharmaceutical Committee
District Nursing Officer
Director of Nursing Services with responsibility for Community Services
Health Education Officer

Local authority: Director of Social Services
Director of Education
Director of Housing
Area Youth Officer

Other agencies: Senior Police Officer
Chief Probation Officer
Disablement Resettlement Officer
Representatives of any street level services
Representative of any rehabilitation house
Representative of any other voluntary organisation working with problem drug takers
Representative of the Manpower Services Commission

Where possible members of the committees should have field-work experience with problem drug takers".

5.19 This composition was intended primarily for the committee's role in developing treatment and rehabilitation; in considering prevention there is

---

* See appendix D for minority view

52

a need for a different emphasis, with wider representation from, in particular, the education sector. The additional membership might include, for example, the following or their nominees on a regular or occasional basis:-

General adviser for health or social and personal education

Officer concerned with education of 16–19 year olds

Head teacher of a secondary school

Head teacher of a primary school

Principal of a college of further education

Representative of any university or higher education establishment

Representative of Community Health Council

Representative of industry or commerce

Representative of any local umbrella organisation for voluntary, self-help or community organizations

Representative of community work in local authorities.

5.20   The exact composition and method of working may vary from place to place and should be determined locally in the light of the needs of the local situation, the extent of the existing involvement of the various statutory and non-statutory agencies, and the need to be able to respond to changing circumstances. The composition we previously recommended included the heads of the most of the relevant services or their nominees and it will be for them to decide which of their staff can make the most effective contribution to the work of the committee in its wider role at any given time. The majority therefore recommend that discussion and implementation of the proposals for the drug advisory committees in the earlier report should take into account our recommendations on the wider role now proposed for them.

5.21   If such a committee, suitably constituted, does not already exist at the appropriate level, it should be the responsibility of certain chief officers, namely, the Director of Social Services, the Director of Education and the District Medical Officer, to ensure that it is set up and continues to function with each discipline making an effective contribution.

5.22   A minority of members of the working group and of the Council have felt unable to agree with the main recommendations made in this section of our report. Their views on co-ordination at regional, district and local level are set out in appendix D.

5.23   Neither the district drug advisory committees nor the alternative proposals set out in the minority report in appendix D will be able to respond with sufficient sensitivity to the needs of individual communities. Their deliberations and activities may provide a framework within which a response can be developed, and may help in that response through the provision of training, expert advice and support, and the supply of materials. The detailed response can however be developed and implemented only by individuals in that community. For example, a problem with the misuse of drugs in a particular school might require co-ordination between the head teacher, the police, the probation service, social services, youth workers, the churches and other voluntary bodies as well as parents. It would be unrealistic to attempt to recommend a formal co-ordinating structure in such circumstances. The best solution must depend both on local needs and on the expertise that may be available.

5.24   We therefore make no specific recommendation, but stress the need for the various agencies concerned to come together at an early stage to agree on what measures of prevention and early intervention might be most appropriate. When such ad hoc groups are established, one of their first priorities should be to ensure that the district drug advisory committee is brought into the picture, both to assist it in monitoring drug problems in its area and to enable it, and the agencies represented on it, to consider ways in which help can be given to the ad hoc group and the community which it serves.

6   Research

6.1   As we stated in our report "Treatment and Rehabilitation" (7), while research on drug misuse in the United Kingdom has made a valuable contribution, there has been insufficient investment. Because of this many crucial questions go unanswered. An earlier report on prevention pointed out that changing harmful life styles will remain the major public health task for the remainder of this century (40). The need to avoid ways of living that increase the risk of disease, accidents and social distress calls for programmes concerned with such matters as exercise, diet, drinking, smoking, driving as well as the responsible use of drugs and where possible the avoidance of misuse. On many of these problems there is an established and substantial research effort but this is not so for drug misuse. The Social Science Research Council has however recently launched a welcome new initiative to promote research into all forms of addiction (41); and the Advisory Council is currently examining its own needs for better information and the extent to which these can be met by research.

6.2   There are, of course, many difficulties for research which sets out to investigate behaviour which not only carries a stigma but may also be illegal. In these circumstances, epidemiological research to establish the prevalence of drug misuse faces problems of ascertainment and reliability of data. Again, evaluating the outcome of prevention programmes raises complicated methodological issues. Such difficulties were discussed in a recent review (42) and in our report "Treatment and Rehabilitation" (7).

6.3   Prevention is concerned with both the supply of and the demand for drugs liable to misuse. Accordingly, this chapter discusses the need for research into the supply of such drugs before reviewing work on the effectiveness of programmes aimed at reducing demand. The need for research into the effectiveness of measures aimed at reducing the harm resulting from drug misuse is also considered, since this too is an aspect of prevention. A substantial part of this report is concerned with the importance of health education in prevention. To match this emphasis it is necessary to review existing knowledge and suggest the framework and design of further studies which would focus upon the evaluation of this type of prevention.

Research on Supply

6.4   The supply of drugs liable to misuse involves sources and channels of differing kinds, legal and illegal, each requiring a number of different stages which range from initial cultivation or production through to eventual prescription or peddling. In chapter 2 we pose some questions about the workings of the illicit drug market at street level (paragraphs 2.17 and 2.18) and we recommend that suitable research studies to elucidate these questions should be carried out. At the other end of the scale we need to improve our understanding of the sources, and this requires international co-operation. For example, the assessment of the effectiveness of crop substitution programmes and the mechanisms of international distribution are seldom the subject of research until the problem becomes relatively 'local' for a supplying or receiving country or even a region of a country. Whilst there have been some studies of those selling illicit drugs, these have been national or local in scope rather than major research supported by international collaboration on the relationship of worldwide supply to demand. Because of variations in definition international data are very unreliable at present, but the international control agencies and the co-operating national agencies know a very great deal about supply, albeit much of it piecemeal and collected from a national, rather than international standpoint. Further, national policies on drug misuse vary over time so that decisions, for example to resume cultivation, have on occasion been based upon political considerations. Unlike other fields of inquiry, e.g. poverty or nutrition, there is very little systematic inquiry and virtually no policy research on the role of governments in the supply and regulation of drugs which may be misused. Such studies would, of course, by their nature be complex, but no more so than the investigations into the problems of world wide poverty or over population, which have been the subject of policy studies and are researched nationally and internationally.

6.5   One valuable result of promoting policy research is the widening of perspective to include the realization that an understanding of drug misuse involves considering the actions of governments as well as of individuals. In other fields such studies have sometimes received support from independent foundations uncommitted to existing policies and approaches. An extension of their support to policy research on drug misuse would add a valuable dimension.

6.6 There is also scope for research on the involvement of the pharmaceutical industry in prevention measures. We have already drawn attention (paragraph 4.16) to the existence of strict controls over the advertising to the general public of medicinal products. Of course, much serious misuse comes from medicines available to the public only on prescription, but that should not be offered as a reason why there should be no research on the prevention policies – international and national – of the manufacturers and suppliers of drugs. The industry makes substantial investment in research, much of which goes to the study of the product including its unwanted side effects. Perhaps a little should go to the study of the pharmaceutical industry and its international and national responsibilities in the field of prevention.

6.7 Problems of supply arise also from the control mechanisms society expects doctors to exercise. There has been much research on the prescribing patterns of doctors and again it is a complex subject. A good deal is known about over-prescribing – the likely characteristics of the doctors, their location and general approach to medical practice as well as the prescribing abuses that may arise from the interface between private and state medicine. Another useful area of "supply" research would be that of the effectiveness of the mechanisms the medical profession has established for regulating the over-prescribing of controlled drugs, for example the so-called "voluntary ban" on the prescription of particular drugs.

6.8 Generally, research on the supply of drugs that may be misused is a neglected area. To concentrate so much on the potential user, though understandable, reflects a lack of balance in the research effort.

Research on Potential Demand*

6.9 By contrast, the literature on the evaluation of drug education to reduce demand is extensive. This is particularly so in the United States where, despite cultural differences, there is much of relevance to the

---

*This section of the report is based mainly on work carried out by our member, Mr Michael Power, in connexion with the preparation of a Council of Europe report on prevention (6).

European situation. Research on drug education programmes has mostly been concerned with evaluating their effectiveness in achieving one or more of three objectives: to give knowledge of the dangers; to influence attitudes towards avoiding drug taking; to modify behaviour and so reduce the level of drug use. Whilst workers stress the difficulty of evaluating experimental programmes, reviews of the results are available from several countries and it is possible to select those studies whose methods were reasonably sound, with large enough samples for significant outcomes, "before" and "after" assessments and comparisons with control groups. The research carried out over the past decade might be summarised as follows:-

(a) A number of studies show it is possible to increase knowledge about drugs and their effects (43–47).

(b) Attempts to influence attitudes towards avoiding drug taking show mixed results, with more negative than positive findings. (Positive: 45, 48–49; Negative: 50–54) Recent studies by Dorn referred to earlier in this report have shown that approaches which aim to involve students more in deciding for themselves their attitude to drug use can be effective.

(c) Studies aiming to reduce drug use mostly show no change in level of use, although two report decreased use and one reports increased use (decreased use: 55 and 56; no change in use: 57–61; increased use: 62). One particular thorough study showed some change from the most toxic to less harmful drugs, but otherwise no alteration in levels of use (63).

6.10 It was already clear to some investigators as early as 1974 that the extensive American and Canadian drug education programmes were largely ineffective as a means of preventing misuse (64). A more recent review (65) confirms this assessment:

"Research has demonstrated that while it is relatively easy to increase drug knowledge, it is more difficult to modify attitudes. A number of studies have reported greater changes in knowledge than in attitudes or have reported changes in knowledge unaccompanied by changes in attitude. Clearly the most rigorous test of educational effectiveness involved subsequent drug abuse. By far the largest number of studies have found no effects of drug education upon use. A few have found drug usage to be reduced while others have found it to be increased following drug education".

6.11   However, the approach outlined in chapter 4 of this report will, if followed, promote the development of preventive measures with much broader aims than formerly and a range of new techniques for achieving those objectives. From a research standpoint, the move of health education away from a situation of narrowly defined and limited programmes of drug education creates problems. This is because the soundest test of any health education programme comes from experimentation, based upon its effect upon a target group compared to a control group. Such evaluation is easier if there is a single well documented input together with an unambiguous measure of outcome. By contrast, broad-based health education may be aimed at a mixed community of individuals of all ages and its effectiveness is to be measured over a range of possible improvements in healthy living. However, recent research shows that the evaluation of broad aim programmes is possible (66). An appropriate research design is outlined in appendix F.

Research on Harm Reduction

6.12   An important aspect of prevention considered in this report is the reduction of harm associated with misuse by measures directed at the user rather than the non-user. More research is needed on a number of issues relating to the scope for, and effectiveness of, this type of prevention.

6.13   One set of issues relates to the measures taken to provide help for those at risk of serious dependence. Elsewhere in this report we point out the value of intervention at an early stage in individual cases of drug misuse as a means of preventing the onset of more serious problems (paragraphs 4.19–4.21). In part this depends on the effectiveness and attractiveness of treatment facilities, and we therefore reaffirm here the recommendations in our report "Treatment and Rehabilitation" (7) for studies on the working of the treatment system and on the attitudes of those who do not seek the help they require (paragraph 9.7 and recommendation 38 – see appendix E).

6.14   Outside the context of the treatment system there are a number of other important issues related to reduction of harm, some of which we have highlighted earlier in this report. For example, in chapter 2 we discuss the possible effects which controls on the supply of drugs may have on established misusers, e.g. "switching" (paragraphs 2.13 – 2.15). In chapter 4 we referred to the need to keep a balance between reduction of harm and reduced recruitment of misusers as objectives for education aimed at specific groups (paragraph 4.40). What are the implications of strategies which involve giving advice to professionals and existing misusers about the relative harmfulness of different drugs misused in different circumstances? A further issue is the role of the media in propagating stereotypes of drug dependence which may be internalized by drug misusers and perhaps applied to other substances, e.g. solvents.

6.15   These and similar issues relating to reduction of harm need to be elucidated by suitable research studies. In the first place we need to improve our knowledge of the effectiveness of policies on supply, education and the media aimed at reducing harm. Secondly, the balance between reduction of harm and reduction of levels of misuse should be explored by studies to show whether, and in what circumstances, the relationship between levels of harm and levels of misuse is positively correlated, reciprocal or insignificant.

7 Summary of Conclusions and Recommendations

7.1 The continued increase in the incidence of drug misuse has caused us to review existing preventive measures and to consider whether they can be improved. In our review we have not confined ourselves solely to the misuse of drugs controlled under the Misuse of Drugs Act but have taken into account the fact that there is some over use, if not misuse, of other drugs taken in order to change mood or modify behaviour. We have considered measures which may reduce the risk of an individual engaging in drug misuse, and those which may reduce the harm associated with misuse.

7.2 In chapter 2 we have concluded that drug misuse is a complex social problem for which no single cause or consistent pattern of multiple causes has been identified; the individual, social groups, economic status and other environmental factors, and the availability of drugs must all be taken into account when developing a comprehensive prevention policy.

7.3 The range and nature of current preventive measures have been described in outline in chapter 3. However the complexity of the causation of drug misuse makes it unlikely that any single measure, either existing or new, can on its own be universally effective. In the present state of knowledge any new measures need to be introduced with caution, and fully evaluated alongside existing measures.

7.4 In chapter 4 we have made proposals in respect of future prevention policy. We have drawn attention to the relationship between the prevention of drug misuse and the effects of broad economic and social policy. There is no precise way of quantifying this relationship; nevertheless development of prevention policy should seek to take account of the effects of those broader policies.

7.5 We have not examined in detail the role of statutory controls in the prevention of drug misuse, but consider that these will continue to make an important contribution.

7.6   Our major recommendations in respect of future prevention policy emphasize the role of education. We endorse the current trend away from education concerned solely with drugs towards broader programmes that aim to promote healthy living. We have examined the various educational approaches used in teaching about health and have concluded that all have some value, but that no one approach is suitable for all purposes. Against this background we have considered the education of the community at large, at national, district and local level, and of specific groups. We have concluded that specific campaigns aimed at preventing drug misuse are in general not desirable, and have recommended a number of alternative approaches. Finally in chapter 4, we have examined briefly the training needs of professionals.

7.7   To ensure that the initiatives which we have recommended are acted upon in a co-ordinated way we have made proposals in chapter 5 for more effective co-ordination at national, district and local levels.

7.8   Finally in chapter 6 we have drawn attention to the lack of sufficient research in certain areas, stressed the need for evaluation of preventive measures and made proposals as to how this might be done.

7.9   Our detailed conclusions and recommendations are:-

Future Prevention Policy

Availability of drugs

1.   There is a case for further strengthening the licensing provisions of the Medicines Act 1968 (4.16).

2.   We reaffirm the recommendations in our report "Treatment and Rehabilitation" for strengthening the services available to drug misusers; when implemented these may also help to prevent the recruitment of new misusers (4.17).

3.   We also reaffirm our recommendations in that report in respect of prescribing safeguards; implementation of these should significantly reduce the availability of prescribed drugs on the black market (4.18).

Education of the Community

4.   Drug education should not concentrate solely on factual information about drug misuse, even less present such information in a way that is intended to shock or scare; a balanced approach is needed which focuses more on social and cultural factors (4.25–26).

5. Broad health education campaigns are probably the best means of seeking to prevent drug misuse in the community (4.28).

6. At national level campaigns which encourage appropriate and safe use of medicines may help to prevent many forms of drug misuse (4.29).

7. National campaigns aimed specifically at reducing the incidence of drug misuse should not be attempted (4.30).

8. There is a need for more nationally produced drug education material; bodies which already produce such material are listed in appendix B (4.30).

9. Media coverage of drugs matters needs to be better informed. The bodies listed in appendix C can assist in this task (4.32); local television and radio can play a significant part in educating the community (4.35).

10. District health authorities and local authorities responsible for personal social services and education should assess the needs of their areas, review the availability of resources and develop suitable prevention programmes (4.33).

11. Inter-agency and multidisciplinary liaison and co-operation is crucial, and the general public should be involved in the planning and execution of programmes (4.34).

12. Preventive measures in local communities should be part of a wider objective of achieving a healthier community (4.36); local participation and partnership in the provision of personal social services offer scope for improved prevention (4.37)

13. A survey of local initiatives in response to drug misuse should be compiled (4.38).

Education of specific groups

14. Educational measures directed at specific groups should, as appropriate, seek to reduce recruitment of new illegal drug users and/or harm to those already misusing drugs (4.40).

15. Education about drugs should be integrated into broader frameworks of health and social education (4.41).

16. Young people should not be regarded as the only target group (4.42).

Training of Professionals

17. We reaffirm the recommendations in our report "Treatment and Rehabilitation" in respect of training (4.48).

18. All professionals who are likely to come into contact with drug misusers should receive some basic training to enable them to recognize drug misuse at an early stage and respond appropriately (4.51).

19. The appropriate authorities should ensure that practitioners are released to attend courses of in-service training in prevention (4.51).

20. Training of health professionals in prevention should take into account the need to educate the general public on the proper use of medicines (4.14).

Responsibility for Prevention

21. Better co-ordination of prevention at national and local levels and between these levels is essential if sufficient impetus is to be given to new initiatives (5.1–5.3).

22. A government minister should assume specific responsibility for the co-ordination of policy on prevention of drug misuse at national level (5.6).

23. The Home Secretary should assume that responsibility (5.8).

24. The Home Office should examine ways in which a suitable forum might be established to enable national organizations concerned with the prevention of drug misuse to exchange views and experience (5.9).

25.* There is a need for a body, at a level between central government and the local community, to develop prevention practice and to co-ordinate the activities of the relevant services (5.10). The tasks of this body are set out in paragraphs 5.11 and 5.12.

26.* The proposals in our report "Treatment and Rehabilitation" for the setting up of drug advisory committees form a basis on which to develop a more broadly-based advisory and co-ordinating committee with an extended function in the field of prevention (5.18); discussion and implementation of these proposals should take into account the wider role we now recommend (5.20).

27.* The composition of these committees should include additional membership representing the educational and community care sectors (5.19).

28.* The exact composition and method of working of these bodies should be determined locally in the light of local needs and circumstances (5.20).

29.* It should be the responsibility of Directors of Social Services, Directors of Education and District Medical Officers to ensure the establishment and effective functioning of these bodies (5.17).

Research

30. There is a need for further research on the workings of the illicit drug market, on measures which can affect the supply of drugs and on the role of governments, international agencies and the pharmaceutical industry in controlling the supply of drugs at source (6.4–6.8).

31. Evaluation of broad-aim health and social education programmes is crucial (6.11). We set out a possible research design for such evaluations in appendix F.

---

* These are recommendations of the majority of the working group which prepared this report and of the Council. For the minority view see appendix D.

64

32. Further research on the scope for reducing the harm associated with drug misuse should include studies on the role of the treatment system in early intervention and the potential contribution of policies on control of supply, education and the media (6.12–6.15).

J. C. BLOOMFIELD
Chairman
    Working Group on Prevention

P. H. CONNELL
Chairman
    Advisory Council on the Misuse of Drugs

D. J. HARDWICK
Secretary
Home Office
Queen Anne's Gate
January 1984

Working Group on Prevention

Membership (since 1977 showing existing or former positions of members)

Mr J C Bloomfield, OBE FPS FBOA JP – Community Pharmacist, Past President of the Pharmaceutical Society of Great Britain (Chairman since November 1979).

Mr A Bristow – Vice-Chairman of Leo Burnett–LPE Ltd, member of the Health Education Council's Mass Media and Public Relations Advisory Panel (Chairman until 1979)

Supt H Brown – Cumbria Constabulary (co-opted in 1982).

Mr D Cox – Team Leader of Avenues Unlimited, Tower Hamlets Youth and Community Project.

Miss P B Dempster BSc (Econ) – Deputy Director, Bedford College of Higher Education (member of the Group since 1981).

Miss A Dixon – Social Worker Adviser on Drug Problems, Camden Social Services Department.

Dr N Dorn BSc MA PhD – Assistant Director (Research) of ISDD (the Institute of the Study of Drug Dependence) (co-opted in 1981).

Professor G Edwards MA DM DPM FRCPsych – Consultant Psychiatrist, Director of the Addiction Research Unit, Institute of Psychiatry (member of the Group since 1979).

Mr M Evans – Director of TACADE (the Teachers' Advisory Council on Alcohol and Drug Education) (co-opted in 1982).

Dr W W Fulton OBE FRCGP – General Practitioner, Glasgow.

Mrs A Jones – Head Teacher of Cranford Community School.

Professor W I N Kessel MD FRCP FRCP Edin FRCPsych – Dean of the Medical School, University of Manchester (member of the Group until December 1980).

Dr B B Lloyd MA DSc – Director, Oxford Polytechnic, Chairman of the Health Education Council (member of the Group until December 1980).

Det Supt R Owen – Merseyside Police (member of the Group from 1979 to 1980).

Mr M J Power – Senior Research Fellow, School of Applied Social Studies, University of Bristol.

Miss G M Rickus CBE BA – Director of Education, London Borough of Brent (member of the Group since 1978).

Mr R E Searchfield – Director of SCODA (the Standing Conference on Drug Abuse) (member of the Group until December 1977).

Mr G T Steele MA – Rector of Johnstone High School, Glasgow (member of the Group since 1978).

Sir Robert Bradlaw CBE – Chairman of the Advisory Council on the Misuse of Drugs until December 1981, member ex officio of the Working Group on Prevention.

Dr P H Connell MD FRCP FRCPsych DPM – Chairman of the Advisory Council on the Misuse of Drugs from September 1982, member ex officio of the Working Group on Prevention.

| Secretary: | Mr D G Turner (until 1980) |
| | Mr D J Hardwick |

Assisted by:	Mrs M J Taylor
	Miss C Le Poer Trench
	Mr N Shackleford
	Mrs C Heald
	Miss K Albiston
	Mr R G Yates
	Mr C Hudson
	Mr R M Bradley

Officials

i. *Home Office*

Mr B Bubbear
Mr G de Deney
Miss J Mott
Mr N Nagler
Ms M Shaw

ii. *Department of Health and Social Security*

Mr B Bennett
Dr D Black
Mrs A Blyth
Mr M Brown
Dr D Cahal
Mr D Caygill
Mr D Guerrier
Dr B Hunt
Miss M Mawson
Mrs M Parkinson
Mrs M Pearson
Ms P Scoular
Mrs A Sincock
Dr A Sippert
Mrs J Sutch

iii. *DES*

Mr J Brierley
Mr W Caldow
Mr E Grogan
Mrs M Holmes
Mr K Morris
Mr F Verdon

Appendix B

Sources for Factual and Educational Material Relevant to the Prevention of Drug Misuse

1. *The Institute for the Study of Drug Dependence (ISDD)*
   Kingsbury House
   3 Blackburn Road
   London
   NW6

ISDD maintains a comprehensive reference library on non-medical use of drugs, and produces information leaflets, health and social education materials, and materials for training of professionals. Information on specific topics can be obtained through ISDD's library and information service. Publications include "Druglink" (a quarterly information letter on drug misuse); "Facts and Feelings about Drugs But Decisions about Situations" (a drug education course for use in secondary schools); "Health Careers" (a project-based course of health and social education in which drug, alcohol and solvent misuse are related to work, cultures and leisure); and a new multi-disciplinary in-service training pack for local courses.

2. *The Teachers' Advisory Council on Alcohol and Drug Education (TACADE)*
   2 Mount Street
   Manchester
   M2 SN9

TACADE provides education and training materials primarily related towards the formal education system. Publications include a basic information leaflet ("Drugs Basic Facts") basic teaching material ("Drugs Teaching Pack") and a fuller education course on the misuse of drugs and other substances ("Free to Choose").

3. *The Standing Conference on Drug Abuse (SCODA)*
   Kingsbury House
   3 Blackburn Road
   London
   NW6 1XA

SCODA is the national co-ordinating body for the non-statutory organizations in the field of drug misuse. Its aims are to assist the development of existing organizations, to advise on and support the establishment of additional services, to encourage field research into problems of drug misuse, and to provide a forum for exchange of information and views on the changing pattern of drug misuse. SCODA publications include a six-weekly newsletter, guides to specialist non-statutory services, and a series of Fieldwork Surveys on drug misuse problems and responses to them in different parts of the country.

4. *Release*
   1 Elgin Avenue
   Maida Vale
   London
   W9 3DR

Release offers advice on the legal and non-legal consequences of drug misuse, and publishers drug education material primarily oriented towards those who are already misusing drugs.

5. *Lifeline Project*
   Joddrell Street
   Manchester
   M3 3HE

Lifeline is a day centre for drug misusers which produces printed and audiovisual training material on drugs and solvent sniffing and possible responses in practice. It is also in process of collaborating on setting up a regional training unit.

6. *The Health Education Council (HEC)*
   Education and Training Division
   78 New Oxford Street
   London
   WC1A 1AH

The HEC's activities are directed mainly towards general health and social education (paragraph 3.11). It has supported several projects on development of curricula and materials for health and social education in schools, and many of these projects touch on legal and illegal drugs. Resource lists on drug, alcohol and smoking education are available from HEC's library. HEC supports Health Education Officers in the field and also supports the training work of TACADE and other agencies. In Scotland similar activities are undertaken by the Scottish Health Education Group.

7. *The Schools Council Health Education Project 12–19*
   Health Education Unit
   Education Department
   Southampton University

The Project prepares material for use in training and by teachers and students. It also assists in training. Drug misuse is among the topics covered.

8. *National Youth Bureau*
   Albion Street
   Leicester

NYB Stimulates innovation in youth work and social education, publishes "Youth and Society", supports regional and local training initiatives for youth workers, and publishes material such as a youth workers' pack on "Enfranchisement" which includes information on the legal aspects of alcohol and drugs.

Appendix C

Sources of Expert Opinion

Additional to those listed in appendix B

In paragraph 4.32 we recommend that the media should make use of expert opinion when preparing articles or programmes in drugs matters. Although it is not possible to make an exhaustive list, the following bodies are among the likely sources of expert opinion on various aspects of drug misuse and its prevention.

The Association of the British Pharmaceutical Industry
12 Whitehall
London SW1A 2DY

The Association of Chief Officers of Probation
20–30 Lawefield Lane
Wakefield WF2 8SP

The Association of Chief Police Officers
New Scotland Yard
London, SW1

The Association of Directors of Social Services
c/o Social Services Department
County Hall
Taunton
Somerset TA1 4DY

The British Medical Association
BMA House
Tavistock Square
London WC1

The Centre for Medicines Research
British Industrial Biological Research Association
Woodmansterne Road
Carshalton
Surrey SM5 4DS

The National Association of Head Teachers
Holly House
6 Paddockhall Road
Haywards Heath
West Sussex RH16 1RG

The National Association of Probation Officers
3 Chivalry Road
London SW11

The National Association of Youth Clubs
16 Strutton Ground
London SW1

The National Council for Voluntary Organisations
26 Bedford Square
London WC1

The National Institute of Social Work
Mary Ward House
5 Tavistock Place
London WC1

The National Union of Teachers
Hamilton House
Mabledon Place
London WC1

The Office of Health Economics
12 Whitehall
London SW1A 2DY

The Pharmaceutical Society of Great Britain
1 Lambeth High Street
London SE1 7JN

The Proprietary Association of Great Britain (represents manufacturers of
medicines on general sale to the public)
519 Victoria House
Southampton Row
London WC1

The Royal College of General Practitioners
14 Princes Gate
London SW7 1BR

76

The Royal College of Physicians
11 St. Andrews Place
Regents Park
London NW1

The Royal College of Psychiatrists
17 Belgrave Square
London SW1

The Secondary Heads' Association
29 Gordon Square
London WC1

The Society Education Officers
5 Bentinck Street
London W1H 5RN

Minority Statement on paragraphs 5.10–5.22

In our view, the problem with the majority's recommendations on the drug advisory committees lies not with those recommendations *per se,* but with the unsuccessful attempts to grapple with difficulties associated with the framework of the relation between the proposed (broad and multidisciplinary) drug advisory committees, and the (opiate treatment services focused) regional drug problem team already proposed in the Council's published report "Treatment and Rehabilitation".

1. THE MAJORITY PROPOSALS

The majority proposals on co-ordination of services related to prevention of drug related problems refer to national, regional (ie health service region), and more local areas.

1.1 *National Level*

We are in accord with the majority proposals on co-ordination at national level (paragraph 5.4 onwards). Firstly, we agree that some greater degree of co-ordination and clarification of statutory and non-statutory action at national level is desirable in relation to the prevention of drug related problems. Secondly, we subscribe to the view that co-ordinating responsibilities should be allocated to the most appropriate agency.

In the case of the prevention of drug related problems, the underpinnings of control rest with statutory measures designed to restrict the supply of and demand for drugs (eg as specified in the Misuse of Drugs Act 1971). These statutory controls on availability form the fundamental basis upon which sit other aspects of prevention policy, such as community prevention and education (discussed in this report). As in other fields (such as drink, diet, health and safety, and environmental pollution) health services, welfare, educational and like measures are *supporting* measures – they do not (and cannot) constitute the basis of control. We agree that the Home Office is the appropriate co-ordinating agency at national level.

79

The Working Group's valuable insights – into the central importance of controls on availability, the danger of planning prevention policy and services too closely around ill-health thinking, and the importance of a community-focused approach to health promotion and education – need to be carried through, from the recommendations for co-ordination at the national level, to recommendations relating to co-ordination at sub-national (regional and more local) levels. The report proposes a Home Office 'top tier' of co-ordination at national level, with a NHS sponsored 'bottom tier' at local level – and silence about the relation between these tiers.

1.2 Practical Problems Below National Level

The majority proposals refer to local (district-level) co-ordination by broadened versions of the drug advisory committees (DACs) previously recommended in the Council's report "Treatment and Rehabilitation". This aspect of the majority proposals appear, if taken in isolation, quite similar to constructive suggestions which we endorse under 3.2 below. But the DACs are envisaged as fitting into a regional structure which has definite implications for prevention locally (Treatment and Rehabilitation, pp. 38–40). Explicit mention is made of training, education, liaison with specialist (ie drug user-focused) and non-specialist agencies, and acting as a catalyst in the development of services 'and as a means of achieving co-ordination of this development' (p.40). This wide educational, training and co-ordinating role is allocated to a regional drug problem team consisting of "the staff of a specialist service, usually a (drug dependence) treatment clinic where one exists", and headed by a consultant psychiatrist (Treatment and Rehabilitation p.39). The Working Group on Prevention has not found a way to reconcile these existing clinical commitments, with good practice in community prevention and education.

The attempted compromise represented in paragraph 5.13 of the report – "we do not see the need for a co-ordinating body at a regional level" – confuses the question of the level of co-ordination, with the question of whether it should be clinically focused or a multidisciplinary partnership of statutory and voluntary agencies.

It is difficult to imagine how the system of co-ordination of drug prevention, implied in these two reports, could function in practices:-

National level: basis of policy is restrictions on availability: co-ordination of prevention debates by Home Office.

80

Regional level:	basis of policy is expansion of drug dependence clinic system; co-ordination of prevention by the clinic (according to the Treatment and Rehabilitation Report), or no policy on co-ordination except a general call for 'good liaison' (according to the Working Group on Prevention).
Local level:	basis of policy is multidisciplinary/community co-ordination; co-ordination by broadened drug advisory committees, including probable membership of the regional drug problem team.

Such a system of co-ordination would have no clear 'vertical' lines of communication, and would not help stimulate the flow of information as envisaged in paragraph 5.3 of this report. It is not difficult to conceive of a more effective system.

2. AN ALTERNATIVE APPROACH EMPHASIZING GENERIC SOCIAL WELFARE/PREVENTION SERVICES AND PARTNERSHIP BETWEEN STATUTORY AND VOLUNTARY SECTORS

2.1 *Generic Services*

We believe that prevention of drug related problems should continue to be regarded as one strand in the broader debate about prevention, health services, health and social education, community development and involvement etc. Government departments and national non-statutory agencies might be asked to make observations about development and co-ordination of *generic* prevention policies and practices – rather than siphoning drug related prevention off into a more specialized drug problem management system. Examples of action that might follow include:- the setting up of more, accessible, medical centres (like that at Great Chapel Street, London); extension of recent and important initiatives on health promotion involving specialists in community medicine, regional administrators and others (eg. Wessex Positive Health Team, West Midlands Health Promotion Group); expansion of advice agencies and housing facilities; development of in-school and public education programmes in which drug (and alcohol) problems are related to decision-making, families, working life and local cultures; in-service training in drug related issues as these arise in the work of generic health, social welfare and education practitioners, etc.

2.2 Statutory/Voluntary Partnership

Insofar as it is necessary to maintain or expand elements of the specialized drug management system, we support the SCODA response to the DHSS on the Council's report on treatment and rehabilitation. This puts forward detailed proposals which include regional development groups to parallel the work of a national development group and to stimulate a community approach, based on developing the resources of a community, not on enhancing the role of a particular agency. The corresponding district body might be quite similar in constitution to that proposed by the majority (paragraphs 5.18.21 above), but the regional/national structure of which it would form a part gives it a much broader role, less clinically focused, and more capable of drug prevention work in the local community and of fitting into a coherent national system.

2.3 Importance of Social Education and its Coordination

The methods of social education and community work that have been developed in youth work, schools and further education, intermediate treatment (in social work departments and voluntary agencies) and, most recently, in youth training for working life are in some respects more realistic than methods characterising most current health education. We commend current practice and debate around social education as a useful resource for the development of more effective approaches to drug/alcohol/solvent education. The fullest development of these resources requires a coherent and truly multidisciplinary co-ordinating framework at local, regional (the precise details of responsibility and coterminosity vary between parts of the UK) and national levels, with education, welfare, health and voluntary agencies working in true partnership at every level.

3. FUNDING

3.1 We believe that drugs, alcohol and solvent sniffing prevention activities that are mounted within and as integral parts of day-to-day customs, policing, health, social welfare, community work, and educational practices should be resourced by the budgets of these agencies. This approach to funding facilitates the development of the most appropriate (non- 'drug specialist') management structures, working practices, and systems of accountability and evaluation.

3.2 Where there is a need for a drug problem focused service (eg along the lines suggested by SCODA), then this service will require long-term finance if it is to develop a viable (ie properly planned, executed and monitored) prevention policy and practice. The danger of short-term 'pump-priming' exercises is that they lead to a concentration on angling for funds, to a period of uncertainty followed by retraction of services, and this is clearly an inefficient use of public funds. An example can be found in the alcohol field, wherein short-term pump-priming money from the DHSS was used to stimulate specialist projects that were expected to be taken over by local government and/or charitable funding. These arrangements have had a dismal history, and we can observe that locally available financial resources are today less available than in previous years, rendering such a funding strategy even more impracticable than hitherto.

4. CONCLUSION

We support the majority proposals on Home Office co-ordination of prevention policy at national level, and the spirit of the proposals on local and community approaches. But we consider that these are incompatible with an *a priori* commitment to regional co-ordination by opiate treatment clinics, and that the resulting system cannot be said to offer clear lines of communication or a basis for 'vertical co-ordination' (national level to local level) in drug prevention policy and practice. We therefore recommend that the alternative structures for co-ordination of policies and activities designed to prevent drug-related problems, described above, should be carefully considered; and we recommend further attention to funding strategy.

D. COX
N. DORN
M. EVANS
G. M. RICKUS
D. TURNER

Textual references

Advisory Council on Misuse of Drugs, 1982, *Treatment and Rehabilitation,* London: HMSO.

Standing Conference on Drug Abuse (SCODA), 1983, *Response to the report from the Advisory Council on the Misuse of Drugs on Treatment and Rehabilitation,* London: SCODA, 27 pages.

Other Reference
National Youth Bureau/various authors, *Youth in Society* (whole issue on 'Social Education Revisited' including practice in MSC settings), 50, January; pp 6–24

Summary of Conclusions and Recommendations of the Advisory Council's Report "Treatment and Rehabilitation"

11.1   In chapter 2 of this report, we have described the historical background to the present services for drug misusers and have concluded that in many instances recommendations made for improving them have never been fully implemented, due in part to the lack of any effective machinery to achieve this. The services themselves have been described in chapter 3 and our analysis of them in chapter 4 has demonstrated that they are now less able than ever to cope with the problems of drug misuse.

11.2   All the indicators point to a substantial increase in the numbers of people misusing drugs. That misuse extends from the opioids through amphetamines and barbiturates to the minor tranquillisers. The increase in multiple drug misuse has been a matter of particular concern to us. In parallel with this growth in drug misuse, there has been increasing questioning of the practice of prescribing controlled drugs to addicts especially on a long-term maintenance basis.

11.3   We have also noted the growing difficulties in finding adequate funds to maintain existing services, particularly by non-statutory agencies, but also by statutory agencies.

11.4   This analysis of the current situation has led us in chapter 5 to propose a move away from the present approach which is largely substance or diagnosis centred towards a problem oriented approach similar to that in the field of alcohol where the term problem drinker has now been adopted. Thus when we use the term problem drug taker we mean any person who experiences social, psychological, physical or legal problems related to intoxication and/or regular excessive consumption and/or dependance as a consequence of his own use of drugs or other chemical substances (excluding alcohol and tobacco).

11.5   It follows from this that we consider that services should be developed in a way which will enable them to respond to the needs of the problem drug taker. The aim must be to provide a range of treatment modules within a long-term perspective. It is this element of matching the individual's needs with service responses which we consider is most lacking in United Kingdom services at present. The main objective must be to utilise not only the full range of specialist services, but also the existing statutory services concerned with social support, including social work and youth services, housing and employment agencies. We must aim to use and build upon the resources we have with imagination and care and to bring co-ordination and consistency to services for problem drug takers.

11.6   We have therefore recommended in chapter 6 the establishment, using existing resources as far as possible, of regional and district drug problem teams and of district drug advisory committees which together can ensure the co-ordinated development of services suited to local needs and can make available specialist advice and support for those working with problem drug takers. Within this framework we make recommendations on the future role of agencies providing services for problem drug takers.

11.7   In chapter 7 we have paid particular attention to the concern at the increasing involvement of doctors working away from hospital-based services in general practice (both NHS and private) and in other forms of private practice and to the risks inherent in this unplanned development. We have concluded that while there may be a role for some of these doctors in the treatment of problem drug takers, there is also a need to ensure that this role is consistent with good medical practice, and that adequate support is available to enable a multi-disciplinary response to be made to the needs of their patients.

11.8   The development of services will require improved training for those likely to come into contact with drug misusers. In chapter 8 we have drawn attention to the lack of training related to drug misuse in professional courses, and to the dearth of specialist training programmes on this subject. We make recommendations which we hope will improve this worrying situation.

11.9   While we consider that it should not be given priority over the provision of services there is a clear need for more research into the treatment and rehabilitation services provided for problem drug takers, along the lines proposed in chapter 9.

11.10   One of the major concerns has been the funding of services. The present arrangements, particularly in the non-statutory sector, are complex and uncertain. If there is to be an adequate response to the undoubted increase in problem drug taking then additional funding must be made available both at local level and from central government.

11.11 Against this background we make the following specific recommendations:

Central/Local Responsibilities

1. There should be no changes at national level in the current allocation of responsibility for policy on services but the arrangements for central government to give advice and support to local agencies should be expanded (6.46–6.51).

2. The new arrangements to improve the accountability of the National Health Service should be used as one means of achieving implementation of our recommendations (6.52).

3. Prime responsibility for the provision and development of services should remain at local level (6.2 and 10.14).

Development of Services

4. In developing services full use should be made of existing resources (6.4).

5. Each regional health authority should ensure that the extent of problem drug taking in its region is monitored, assess the extent of the services provided and develop a policy for meeting local needs. (6.6).

6. Each regional health authority should establish a multi-disciplinary regional drug problem team (6.6).

7. Regional drug problem teams should have a permanent identifiable base, usually a designated treatment clinic, or another existing specialist service where one exists (6.8).

8. Apart from providing a specialist service, the regional drug problem teams should have a peripatetic role within the region, giving support and advice to, and liaising with specialist and non-specialist agencies and encouraging the development of new services (6.9).

9. Within three years, drug advisory committees should be established in the majority of health districts to monitor the extent of problem drug taking, assess the effectiveness of existing services and to foster their improvement (6.11 and 6.12).

10. Membership of the drug advisory committees should include representatives of health and local authorities and other statutory and non-statutory agencies (6.14).

11. In the longer term each health district should establish a team similar to but broader in composition than the regional drug problem teams (6.15 and appendix G).

12. As the advisory committees and district teams become established the regional teams should concern themselves more with long-term strategy for the development of services (6.16).

13. Relevant statistical data held by central government should be made available to drug advisory committees and regional drug problem teams while preserving confidentiality (6.20).

The Role of Individual Agencies

14. Hospital-based treatment services should encompass the treatment of all forms of problem drug taking (6.23).

15. The minimum nucleus of such a service should comprise a consultant psychiatrist, with either a senior registrar, registrar or clinical assistant, as well as a social worker, nurse and secretary, who should have had special training and experience. The consultant should either have charge of or access to beds in an inpatient unit and laboratory facilities should be available (6.24).

16. The minimum functions of a clinic should include the acceptance of problem drug takers as patients from a variety of referral sources preferably from their general practitioner for assessment, with options of help from different disciplines, in liaison with other services (6.25).

17. Advisory/counselling services should be developed and might be combined with day care centres (6.31 and 6.33).

18. A wider range of residential facilities is needed and their development should include a greater degree of flexibility in the programmes offered and in the length of stay (6.34 and 6.35).

19. The expertise and methods of working introduced by the non-statutory agencies should be borne in mind when services are developed (6.36).

20. Local authority social services should consider ways of promoting their involvement in developing services (6.40).

21. Structured hostel provision should be made available to organisations working with problem drug takers by means of management agreements with housing associations (6.44).

Prescribing Safeguards

22. A network of support based on the regional drug problem teams should be available to doctors not working in hospital-based services who are treating problem drug takers; where necessary such doctors should liaise with hospital-based services and should utilise the services of other disciplines; and opportunities should be created for them to develop their knowledge and understanding of drug problems (7.18 and 7.19).

23. Guidelines should be prepared on good medical practice in the treatment of problem drug takers (7.24).

24. As a matter of urgency, the ability to prescribe dipipanone, and therefore Diconal, to addicts should be restricted to doctors licensed by the Secretary of State (7.27).

25. This licensing restriction should also be extended at the earliest possible date to all other opioids, such extension being considered urgently in conjunction with the preparation of guidelines for good practice (7.32).

26. The Government should consider as a matter of urgency ways of fulfilling the original intention that the Misuse of Drugs Act should be able to deal with all forms of irresponsible prescribing, ranging from serious professional misconduct at one extreme to poorly judged but bona fide intention at the other (7.38).

Training

27. Consideration should be given to developing training about drugs, alcohol, solvents and tobacco in an integrated way, particularly for those working with the young (8.10).

28. The appropriate professional bodies should review the provision of education regarding drug problems in pre-qualification courses (8.12), and explore ways in which education and training about problem drug taking might be included in post-basic qualification courses (8.13).

29. Employers of residential staff should consider ways of providing in-service training (8.14).

30. The appropriate professional bodies and national training agencies should examine the pre- and post-qualification courses for residential staff and should ensure the inclusion of education about drug problems in their curricula (8.14).

31. More in-service training should be provided at local level both for particular professional groups and for multi-disciplinary groups (8.15 and 8.16).

32. Training and education in drug problems should be designed and provided specifically for senior and middle managers (8.8 and 8.17).

33. The Health Departments should establish one or more intensive multi-disciplinary courses for trainers involving supervision over at least six months (8.18).

34. The Health Departments should consider ways in which the need for multi-disciplinary expertise and training might be met including the possible establishment of a national training facility (8.20 and 8.21).

35. Local training courses should be considered for pump priming funding by central government (8.22).

36. The need for financial provision to be allocated for the training of staff in non-statutory agencies should not be overlooked (8.23).

37. Training provision should be reviewed from time to time jointly by the appropriate government departments and the national professional bodies (8.24).

Research

38. Further research is needed into service policy, techniques and processes of treatment and rehabilitation, and the factors which influence problem drug takers to seek help (9.4–9.7).

39. New mechanisms are needed to ensure that such research is initiated (9.3).

40. The need for research should not delay help for the problem drug taker, but the monitoring and evaluation of new and existing services is important (9.10).

Funding

41. There may be a need to redirect current resources towards services for problem drug takers, and priorities should be reviewed (10.4).

42. Funds should be provided primarily from local sources, most probably from joint funding arrangements (10.14).

43. There should be increased funding direct from central government possibly by way of pump priming grants normally for a minimum period of 5 years (10.16).

44. Consideration should be given to the issuing by central government of guidelines to health and local authorities on the provision of funds (10.17).

45. Ways of funding services should be reviewed urgently, taking into account the special factors which affect provision for problem drug takers (10.18).

Appendix F

Suggested Evaluation Research Design

Stage I

1. *The Pilot programme*

A new health education programme aimed at modifying life styles would regard the first attempt as a *pilot to establish the acceptability and relevance of its content.* At this stage the evaluator works closely with those responsible for the programme and also with others who are participating. The research design is shaped by the aims and views of all concerned. With this in mind at this stage an anthropological approach is helpful aiming, as described by one investigator, at: "knowing and understanding others through sympathetic introspection and reflexion from detailed description and observation" (67). In the light of this pilot experience the programme may be modified and re-tested. In this manner a pattern of "action, reaction and adaptation" is established until those concerned, practitioners, researchers and the community are all satisfied that the content and mode of delivery can really engage the interest of the group, young, middle-aged, or old who are most vulnerable to possible misuse.

2. *Aims*

After this the "running" programme is ready for *experimental testing.* As a result of the initial exploration it should be possible to be more specific about setting realistic targets to achieve healthier ways of life including minimum levels of necessary drug use and steps to avoid misuse. This should be attempted by using a group approach with membership from all sections of a community. It would include key people in the local neighbourhood, such as estate caretakers, the sub-postmaster, the organisers of voluntary action, the teachers, doctors, nurses, social workers in primary care, the youth and community workers and school students, together with staff from day care facilities for all age groups.

3. *Comparison*

(i) This next step requires a new district with a group not previously involved in the development work of the education for health programme. All entering the programme should be interviewed to establish their knowledge of risk factors, their attitudes towards health care, and their degree of interest in changing to healthier ways. Only *after* such an *initial screening* should they be *allocated randomly* either to an experimental group to share in the new programmes, or to a control group. At this point it should then be established whether or not these groups share comparable characteristics for age, sex, knowledge, attitudes and motivation etc.

(ii) The size of the groups can be crucial in establishing possible significant differences in outcome. Because of the multiple inputs and objectives most work of this type requires a reasonably large experimental group. Statistical advice, although important from the very beginning is vital at this stage to determine the "end-points" and then establish, for different levels of significance, the numbers required.

(iii) However, sometimes random allocation is not feasible, for example because students in the same class or next door neighbours may find themselves in different groups. In this way, friends may inadvertently share the new health education approach informally, and by such "contamination" reduce the vital differences between experimental and control groups during the programme. This is especially the case with lengthy broad-aim health education that has to make a major impact in order to shift behaviour. In these circumstances a quasi-experimental design may permit a comparison of similar districts or schools rather than of two randomly selected groups of individuals. In this way, it is more likely that all who are likely to know each other can follow the same health education regime. However, it is important to recognize that such a course reduces the power of the design to produce comparable experimental and control groups for whom other influences will not operate selectively (for example, major changes during the experiment in one school only of policies over pastoral care may have an "institutional" effect and may operate differently between groups). The inability to hold constant all factors likely to influence the outcome make such experiments difficult and the preferred design remains that of random allocation if at all practicable.

4. *Monitoring the health education*

It is important to monitor the experiment closely. This *process evaluation* checks actual practice against the experience of the pilot stage, and establishes how far on this occasion it departs from the stated aims of the programme. Should at the end it be possible to establish differences in outcome between experimental and control groups, a detailed account of the actual input (not just the plan at the beginning) becomes crucial if any benefits are to be used elsewhere. In this way, such projects can be repeated in an attempt to eliminate the inevitable chance factors that may happen only once. *Replication,* an important strategy for evaluative research, should if possible be attempted.

5. *Repeat Measurement*

At the end of the programme, the subjects should be screened again for movement on the initial measures. Such *pre-post* designs are standard and necessary to establish the status of the groups immediately before and after administering the programmes. Should undue delay occur at either point other factors may intervene to substantially alter the measures. However, it may be that the impact of the programme is "slow acting", or, if immediate, very short-lived. In either case, a *follow-up* of both experimental and control groups helps to eliminate false conclusions.

6. *Follow-up*

Another problem at this stage is the attrition due to the normal mobility of families in most industrialised societies. For example, if the programme lasts throughout a school year, perhaps as many as 15% of students and teachers may have left. Similarly, 10% of the residents in a district may move elsewhere within a year. However, recent feasibility studies of follow up of mobile groups of young people showed that most of them could be traced and contacted (68, 34). The required length of follow up will vary according to the content of the education for health programme. If for example, the programme aims to avoid or retard the onset of cigarette smoking or, at later ages, cannabis use, a two year follow up may be long enough, whilst reduction of alcohol consumption or avoiding completely opiate use may require different follow up periods. With broad-aim programmes subjects cannot be contacted too frequently and a follow up plan is important before the experiments start rather than as a hurried after-thought.

List of References

(1)   International Narcotics Control Board, *Report for 1982;* Vienna, United Nations, 1983.

(2)   Triesman, D et al., *A Survey to Estimate the Number of Cannabis Users in the UK* (commissioned by BBC Midweek), London, Social Research and Design Consultancy, 1973. See also ISDD Library and Information Services, *Surveys and Statistics on Drug Taking in Britain,* London, ISDD, 1983.

(3)   Home Office Statistical Bulletin 13/83; Home Office, July 1983.

(4)   DHSS, *Treatment and Rehabilitation: Report of the Advisory Council on the Misuse of Drugs;* HMSO, 1982 (paragraph 4.5).

(5)   Study on measures to reduce illicit demand for drugs: Preliminary Report of a Working Group of Experts; United Nations, 1979.

(6)   Council of Europe, European Public Health Committee: *The Prevention of Drug Dependence;* Strasbourg, Council of Europe, 1982.

(7)   DHSS, *Treatment and Rehabilitation: Report of the Advisory Council on the Misuse of Drugs;* HMSO, 1982.

(8)   Advisory Council on the Misuse of Drugs, *Drug Misuse Among Children of School Age;* DES, 1977.

(9)   Plant, M, *"Drugtaking and Prevention: The Implications of Research For Social Policy;"* British Journal of Addiction, 1980. For an exhaustive review of the world literature, see Fazey, C, *The Aetiology of Non-Medical Drugs Use;* Paris, Unesco, 1976.

(10) See for example: Plant, M, *Drug Takers in an English Town;* Tavistock, 1975; Graham, H, *"Smoking in Pregnancy"; Social Science and Medicine,* 1976, 10, pp 399–405; Dorn, N, *"Alcohol in Teenage Cultures"; Health Education Journal,* 1982, 39, pp 67–73; Auld J, *Cannabis and Social Control;* Academic Press, 1981.

(11)   Dorn, N and Thompson, A, *A Comparison of 1973 and 1974 levels of mid teenage experimentation with illegal drugs in some schools in England;* ISDD, 1975. See also Becker, H, *Outsiders;* Free Press, 1966 (especially chapter 3).

(12)   There is debate about the precise nature of the relationships between availability and consumption of alcohol; see for example: Tuck, M, *Alcoholism and Social Policy;* HMSO, 1980; and the response by Skog, O, *"Alcoholism and Social Policy: Are We On The Right Lines?";* British Journal of Addiction; 1981, 76, pp 315–321.

(13)   Gooberman, L, *Operation Intercept: The Multiple Consequences of Public Policy;* Pergamon Press, 1974.

(14)   See for example the evidence and discussions in Plant, M, (op cit) and Fazey, C, (op cit) but note recent resurgence of interest in the concept of escalation: O'Donnell, J and Clayton, R, *"The Stepping Stone Hypothesis";* Chemical Dependencies, 1982, 4, 3, pp 229–241.

(15)   It is possible that, with employment and legitimate small businesses, the so-called "informal economy" of casual work and exchange may expand, the market in illicit drugs being part of this "informal economy" (Dorn, N and South N, *"Sociology and Dangerous Drugs – Coming Full Circle"* (book review); British Journal of Addiction, 1982, 77, pp 322–5.

(16)   See for example Plant, M, (op cit).

(17)   CPRS, *A Joint Framework for Social Policies;* HMSO, 1975.

(18)   DHSS, *Prevention and Health: Everybody's Business;* HMSO, 1976 and *Inequalities in Health;* HMSO, 1980.

(19)   Ministry of Health and the Department of Health for Scotland; *Drug Addiction: Report of the Interdepartmental Committee;* HMSO, 1961.

(20)   Ministry of Health and Scottish Home and Health Department; *Drug Addiction: The Second Report of the Interdepartmental Committee;* HMSO, 1965.

(21)   See for example: Grey Advertising, *Grey Matter;* London, 1970, for the use of media campaigns in the USA; and in contrast, Dorn, N, *Social Analyses of Drugs in Health Education and the Media;* in Edwards, G, and Busch, C, *Drug Problems in Britain;* Academic Press, 1981.

(22) Golding, P, *The Mass Media;* Longman, 1974.

(23) McCron, R, and Budd, J, *Mass Communication and Health Education;* in Sutherland, J, (ed), *Health Education: Perspectives and Choices;* Allen & Unwin, 1979. Also Dorn, N, and South, N, *Message in a Bottle,* Chapter 2; Gower Press, 1983.

(24) DES, *Health Education in Schools;* HMSO, L977.

(25) Triesman, D, (op cit).

(26) *Prevalence of Psychotropic Drugtaking Amongst Women in the UK;* ISDD, Unpublished.

(27) Perry, L, *Women and Drug Use: An Unfeminine Dependence;* ISDD, 1979.

(28) ISDD, *Bibliography on Womens' Use of Legal and Illegal Drugs;* 1981.

(29) Advisory Council on the Misuse of Drugs, *Report on a Review of the Classification of Controlled Drugs and of Penalties under Schedules 2 and 4 of the Misuse of Drugs Act 1971;* Home Office 1979.

(30) Advisory Council on the Misuse of Drugs, *Security of Controlled Drugs;* Home Office, 1983.

(31) Payne, D, *"The Relationship between Television Advertising and Drug Abuse among Youth: Fancy and Fact";* Journal of Drug Education 1976, vol 6(3).

(32) Drug and Therapeutic Bulletin – 1976, 14, p.65.

(33) Norwegian Medicinal Goods and Poisons Act 1964, para 14.

(34) See for example: Schaps, E et al., *"A review of 127 Drug Abuse Prevention Program Evaluations"; Journal of Drug Issues,* 1981 vol 11 no 1. (Programme strategies based on information and persuasion alone generally received low evaluations.)

(35) Community Service Volunteers, *CSV and Social Action Broadcasting.*

(36) Council of Europe, European Public Health Committee, (op cit), chapter 4.

(37) Hadley, R, and McGrath, M, (eds), *Going Local: Neighbourhood Social Services;* Bedford Square Press, 1980.

(38) National Institute of Social Work, *Social Workers: Their Role and*

Tasks; Bedford Square Press for the National Institute Social Work, 1982.

(39) DHSS, *Care in Action: A handbook of policies and priorities for the health and personal social services in England;* HMSO, 1981.

(40) DHSS, *Prevention and Health: Everybody's Business;* HMSO, 1976.

(41) SSRC, *Research Priorities in Addiction: The Report of a Social Science Research Council Sub-Committee;* SSRC, 1982.

(42) Edwards, G and Busch, C (eds.) *Drug Problems in Britain;* Academic Press, 1981.

(43) Smith, B C, *"Values Clarification in Drug Education – a Comparative Study", Journal of Drug Education,* 1973, vol 3, pp 369–376.

(44) Shetler, R H, *A Study of the Value of In-Service Drug Education Training for Teachers;* M S Thesis, Glassboro State college, 1973.

(45) Dorn, N, *The Dede Project;* London, Health Education Council and the Institute for the Study of Drug Dependence, 1977.

(46) Sadler, O W and Dillard, N R, *"A Description and Evaluation of Trends: A Substance Abuse Education Programme for Sixth-Graders"; Journal of Education Research,* 1978 vol 71 pp 171–175.

(47) Manske, S R and Schlegel, R P, *The Comparatie Effectiveness of Three Educational Interventions on Alcohol Attitudes and Behaviours among School Children;* Offset publication, University of Waterloo, Ontario, 1978.

(48) Friedman, S M, *A Drug Education Programme Emphasising Effective Approaches and its Influence upon Intermediate School Student and Teacher Attitudes;* PhD Dissertation, Fordham University, 1973.

(49) Warner, R W Jr., *Evaluation of Drug Abuse Prevention Programmes in* Corder, B W et al. (eds), *Drug Abuse Prevention: Perspectives and Approaches for Education;* Dubuque, 1975.

(50) Cox, C and Smart, R R, *"A Failed Comparison of Structured and Unstructured Approaches to Drug Education" Substudy 2–33;* Toronto: Addiction Research Foundation, 1970.

(51) Degnan, E J, *An Exploration into the Relationship between Depression and a Positive Attitude towards Drugs in Young Adolescents and an Evaluation of a Drug Education programme;* Ed D Dissertation, Rutgers University, 1971.

(52) Kriner, R E and Vaughan, M R, *"The Effects of Group Size and Presentation"*, Technical Report 75–11, ERIC Document Reproduction Service No. ED 112 325; Alexandria, VA: Human Rights Resources Research Organisation, 1975.

(53) Bruhn, J G, Phillips, B V and Coruin, H D. a. *"The Effects of Drug Education Courses on Additional Change in Adult Participants; International Journal of Addictions,* 1975, vol 10 pp 65–96. b. *"Follow up of Adult Participants in Drug Education Courses; International Journal of Addictions,* 10, pp. 241–249.

(54) Morgan, H G and Hayward, A, *"The Effects of Drug Talks to School Children"; British Journal of Addiction,* 1976, vol 71, pp. 285–288.

(55) Carney, R E, *An Evaluation of the 1970–71 Coronado, California, Drug Abuse Education Programme Using the Risk-taking Attitude Questionnarie.* Unpublished Report, 1971.

(56) McCellan, P P, *"The Pulaski Project – an Innovative Drug Abuse Prevention Programme in an Urban High School"; Journal of Psychedelic Drugs,* 1975 vol 7, pp. 355–362.

(57) McClune, D A, *A Study of More Effective Education Relative to Narcotics, other Harmful Drugs and Hallucinogenic Substances: a Progress Report submitted to the California Legislator;* California State Department of Education, Sacramento, 1970.

(58) Sillem, A, *Experimental Underzoeh Naar Effecten van Drugvoorlichting;* Stichting voor Alcohol en Drugunderzoek, Amsterdam, 1974.

(59) Cook, R F and Morton, A S, *"An Assessment of Drug Education – Prevention Programmes in the United States Army"*, Technical Paper 261, ERIC Document Reproduction Service No. ED 106 708; United States Army Research Institute for the Behavioural and Social Sciences, Washington DC, 1975.

(60) De Haes W and Schurman, J, *"Results of an evaluation study of three drug education methods"; International Journal of Health Education,* 1975 vol 18.

(61) Pipher, J R, *An Evaluation of an Alcohol Course for Junior High School Students, and Examination of Differential Course effectiveness as Annotated with Subject Characteristics;* PhD dissertation, University of Nebraska, 1977.

(62) Stuart, R B, *"Teaching Facts about Drugs: Pushing Prevention";* Journal of Educational Psychology 1974, vol 66 pp. 189–201.

(63) Blum, H, Blum, E and Garfield, E, *Drug Education – Results and Recommendations;* Lexington, MA: DC Health, 1976.

(64) Goodstadt, M ed., *Research on methods and programmes of Drug Education;* Addiction Research Foundation, Ontario, 1974.

(65) Hanson, D J, *Drug Education – does it work?;* in Scarpitti, F and Datesman, S, (eds). *"Drugs and Youth Culture"* Sage Annual *Reviews of Drug and Alcohol Abuse,* 4, 1980.

(66) Weiss, C H, *Evaluating Action Programmes: Readings in Social Action and Education;* Allyn and Bacon, Boston, 1972.

(67) Pattern, M.Q, *Utilization-Focused Evaluation;* Beverley Hills CA., Sage Publications, 1978.

(68) National Children's Bureau, *The Follow up of young adults born 1958 who were formerly Children in Care;* Report of N.C.B. London, 1980.

Printed in the UK for HMSO
Dd737590 C15 4/85 H P Ltd So'ton (757)